# From Waidale *to the* *world*

# From Waidale *to the world*

The Waidale Missionary Trust 1967–2017

Valmai Redhead

From Waidale to the World
Published by The Waidale Missionary Trust
Gore
New Zealand



ISBN 978-0-473-44258-3 (Softcover)
ISBN 978-0-473-44259-0 (ePUB)
ISBN 978-0-473-44260-6 (Kindle)

Editing: Sue Beguely

Production & Typesetting:
Andrew Killick
Castle Publishing Services
www.castlepublishing.co.nz

Cover Design: Zoë Cromwell
Front cover image: John Gardyne and Richard White
look towards the Gracevale farm.

*Dedicated to my dear mother-in-law, Alice Redhead.
As the book goes to print, she is about to celebrate her
ninety-ninth birthday. She encourages me in my writing
and inspires me with her prayers and her desire to share
God's unconditional love with everyone.*

*She has never written a book.
Instead she has written countless letters
to dozens of missionaries for decades.
She has never gone overseas.
Instead she has stayed and prayed.
This is mission.*

*There are no little people with God.*

– Norman McIntosh

# Foreword

This book is more than the history of an organisation through fifty years. It is a book of people's unique stories. Their lives, serving the Lord through faith, have been woven together to produce the fabric of The Waidale Missionary Trust.

The Trust has been part of my life since childhood. I was only nine years old when Andrew and Margaret Dunn were farewelled but my vivid memories of that day still remain. Hearing Norman McIntosh speak at the tenth anniversary celebration is another moment that has stayed with me. Other recollections have been rekindled through reading this book while some stories were new to me.

I feel inspired by the vision and faithfulness of the original Trustees and their spouses, who, through finances, prayer, letter writing, hospitality and other practical ways have given so much. Continuing to support the work of those who serve in New Zealand and overseas has been a privilege. My life has been enriched through friendships formed and seeing God at work as each generation encouraged by The Waidale Missionary Trust, discovers how their farm or business can be part of their faith journey. Missional business may be new terminology but the concept is not. I am so thankful that God is raising up younger Christian farmers, as trustees and graziers, who continue to enlarge the vision.

My grateful thanks to Valmai for her active, enthusiastic research and her professional approach that has brought this book to fruition. Her regular prompts for meeting deadlines have been both appreciated and necessary. She has enabled these stories of faith to be told.

It is my hope that as you read you will be blessed and inspired in fresh ways in your own journey of serving the Lord.

Graeme Gardyne
Chairman

# Acknowledgements

One person may be named as the author, but it takes many people to produce a book: teamwork makes the dream work. Thank you to:

Graeme Gardyne and the Trust members for having faith in me to complete this task.

Diane and George Cook whose willingness to spend time working alongside me has been pivotal on this journey. There have been many emails, phone calls, and visits to ponder and discuss details. I could not have done this without you.

Zoë Cromwell whose graphic design skills have been greatly appreciated as together, with several of the Waidale Trust members, we have deliberated long and hard over cover design options. Your perseverance and patient endurance deserves a medal.

Averil Bennett, whose appreciation of mission, understanding of Waidale and wise counsel have been a great blessing. Your expertise has been invaluable as I have negotiated my way through a maze of words, quotes and facts to produce a coherent and readable story.

Those I have interviewed in person and to others who have responded to emails. You have each given up time to provide personal stories, describing how Waidale has been part of your life. You have checked what I have written and explained the things I did not understand. Your contributions make this book a rich tapestry of life experience.

The proof readers who have read through the manuscript with meticulous and careful attention to detail. George Cook, Graeme Gardyne and George Simpson have checked information and facts. Averil Bennett, Teresa Blackbeard and Frances Robertson have checked grammar, spelling and layout discrepancies that may have slipped in unnoticed during the publishing process. Though these details may seem small they are very important and your work is appreciated.

Sue Beguely for your professional, competent editing as you ensure every detail in the narrative is honed to a high standard, ready for publishing. It has been such a pleasure to work with you again, knowing you understand and support a vision for mission.

Andrew Killick of Castle Publishing Ltd. Your professional guidance and help throughout the publishing process has been invaluable. Your patience and wisdom is valued. It has been a great pleasure working with you again.

*God has given each of you a gift from His great variety of spiritual gifts. Use them well to serve one another (1 Peter 4:10, NLT).*

# Contents

# Preface

Living in a Southland community where mission is valued and well supported, has consolidated my lifelong interest in mission. I remember the thrill of supporting my first missionary once I started work. My late husband Laurence and I sent out prayer letters for my sister Irelle who spent more than 30 years working in Japan. The task became a family affair, and for our daughter Joanna, it was a commitment that contributed to planting mission in her heart. She now works with a mission business initiative offering freedom to women who have been trafficked into the sex trade.

Hearing guest speakers at events hosted by The Waidale Missionary Trust has expanded my appreciation of the vital role it plays in worldwide mission and being asked to write this history was indeed a privilege. I was given the brief to update the history of the Trust, carrying on work done by George Simpson for the Trust's twenty-fifth anniversary and recorded in 'The Waidale Story'. My contribution would continue the story through to the Trust's fiftieth jubilee. While reading 'The Waidale Story' one phrase captured my attention: 'There are no little people with God'. Norman McIntosh used it when speaking at the tenth anniversary celebrations.

The profound truth of these words (originally attributable to Francis Schaeffer) inspired me. As I interviewed those who have been responsible for shaping and guiding the development of the Trust over the last fifty years, an outstanding testimony emerged of the way in which many unassuming people have been shaped by God for His glory. As I have listened to the stories and understood the connections forged through generations within a strong Christian community network, patterns have emerged: of faithfulness, humility, leadership, enthusiasm and commitment. These qualities are rare within a world that focuses on self-interest and instant gratification. No wonder missionaries love visiting Southland where a strong sense of the presence and the favour of God abounds, together with generous hospitality and meal tables full of fresh farm baking.

Every year the Waidale trustees have to make difficult decisions, because it is not possible to approve funding for all applicants. It has always been their dream that others might be inspired by their model and motivated to emulate the idea. My prayer is that this book might nudge someone else to explore new ways of expanding God's vision for mission in their corner of the world.

Valmai Redhead

# In the Beginning...

***Harry:*** It's another good turnout to the Pounawea Convention this year, Clarence.

***Clarence:*** Yes, yes … and an impressive line-up of missionaries as usual at our mission's afternoon wasn't it?

***Harry:*** Yes … I was most impressed with Andrew and Margaret Dunn.

***Clarence:*** Mmm yes, I was too. It's a crying shame the church isn't able to send them in the foreseeable future though.

***Harry:*** That's got me thinking … I'm sure God's work shouldn't be limited by weakness in our church government and finances at the present time!

***Clarence:*** This Geering controversy certainly isn't helping things.

***Harry:*** I'm thinking that God owns the cattle on a thousand hills …

***Clarence:*** (Laughs) … and Sep Wyma thinks a thousand of them are on one of your hills!

***Harry:*** (Chuckles) Well, not quite a thousand … But think about it, Clarence. We each come from parishes with Christian farmers like ourselves. If each of us fattened some cattle or sheep, and then sold them and the proceeds went into a fund, we could finance Andrew and Margaret ourselves!

***Clarence:*** Ye-es … although stock prices are in decline just at the moment …

***Harry:*** Couldn't be a better time to buy up stock then! Why don't you take the idea to the farmers at Waikaka – I can see people like George Simpson and Bert Gardyne along with others coming on board. And I'll do the same in our Riversdale parish. I'm sure Ron Paterson will be a starter, and Stan Clark and a few others won't take much convincing. Let's see what we come up with.

***Clarence:*** OK. I don't suppose we should let these two clouds limit our vision … Assuming we get enough support to go ahead with this, any ideas on how to organise it?

***Harry:*** Oh, I should think we could form a Trust to administer the funds. The folk who are prepared to graze stock or contribute in some way could be the trustees. We could call it the Riversdale-Waikaka Missionary Trust or something like that.

***Clarence:*** Or the Waikaka-Riversdale Missionary Trust!

***Harry:*** (Chuckles) Either way, it's a bit of a mouthful. We'd have to come up with something better than that I should think!

***Clarence:*** Why not, ah … Why not, um … Why not The Waidale Missionary Trust? That's *wai* from Waikaka and *dale* from Riversdale!

***Harry:*** Yeah … that would work. Better than Riverkaka Missionary Trust! Hmm … yes. The Waidale Missionary Trust. And we'll have Andrew and Margaret Dunn on the mission field before another Pounawea Convention takes place shall we?

(A re-enactment of the perceived conversation between Harry White and Clarence Gardyne as presented by Malcolm White and John Gardyne at the 50th Jubilee celebration. Created by Josephine Dodds.)

# The First Decade

1967–1977

## Two Farmers Meet a Missionary Couple

In Eastern Southland there once lived two farmers. Both had grown up in church, but their lifestyle was not about religion and rules. Rather, it was like a partnership with a God who was interested in farming just like they were. They were very different and yet they had much in common.

**Clarence Gardyne** was not a big man. You might not notice him in a crowded room, but he was known as a man of principle and integrity, a humble man who gave his word and stood by it. His character had grown with him. Over the years he had developed a good work ethic. As the eldest of four children, he had learnt a great deal about farming from his father, William.

The Gardyne family had farmed in the Chatton district in Eastern Southland since 1876 when grandparents Robert and Elizabeth bought land in the area. The 460-acre (186 ha) property was a mixed farm providing a good balanced income. William had succeeded his father and had farmed well, but the war and his failing health took its toll. Crippling arthritis reduced his mobility and made physical work difficult, so it was with great reluctance

Clarence left school in his mid-teens and undertook responsibility not only for the farm, but for the staff working there. His father, in his sixties, gave him guidance and instructions but nevertheless it was a big step. Gradually, as his confidence grew, Clarence began to make changes.

Some of the farm buildings were getting old and needed replacing. Upgrading equipment was a priority. A bulk header and a drier were purchased enabling the harvest process to be much more efficient. Initially the grain still needed to be bagged because Fleming's Creamoata Mill in Gore did not have the machinery to process bulk grain but, thankfully, they upgraded a couple of years later. Clarence worked steadily to improve production and capacity on the farm. In 1970 he bought an additional 300 acres (121.4 ha). His boys, Graeme and John, grew up learning farming from their dad. He was generous, but also believed that a hand-up was wiser than a handout. He enabled his sons, then aged 21 and 23, to purchase the neighbouring farm, Carslae. Today John still farms there, while Graeme owns the home block. Like his father before him, approximately half of Graeme's returns are from sheep and beef while the other half comes from cropping.

The Gardyne family were committed Christians. As Clarence grew up he attended church with them every Sunday. His grandmother, Elizabeth, was one of the earliest members of the Knapdale Presbyterian Church. The church stood on land donated by Alexander McNab, an early pioneer and major runholder in Eastern Southland. Elizabeth's journey of faith began at the time of the Knapdale revival that saw unprecedented growth in church attendance. The revival began on New Year's Day 1881 when Scottish settler James Dickie was deeply convicted by the words he was reading in the gospel of John. God's unmistakable power transformed his whole being and he rose from his prayerful devotion as a changed man. With zeal and enthusiasm he began to share his experience with others, who in turn were convicted of their need to turn to God. The influence reverberated throughout the district for years, touching many families including the Gardynes.

When Clarence reached his teenage years, attending Bible Class was a rite of passage. Lifelong friendships were formed, especially at camps which were an annual highlight. At one such Easter camp he was deeply impacted by the passionate, strong preaching of the blind evangelist, Andrew Johnston. He made a decision to commit his life and his future to God. Later, he taught Sunday school at Knapdale for many years. But his faith was not something kept only for Sunday. Every part of his life was increasingly influenced by biblical principles. Graeme remembers the example his parents set of having Bible reading and prayer every morning in their bedroom before they got up to start the day. His dad would also pray for people as he drove down the road (with eyes open, of course!)

Farming is known for its seasonal cycles of plenty and want, underpinned by climatic factors and trading prices, but Clarence worked hard through every season to provide for his family. Their meal table was a great place for robust conversation. He was caring towards his staff and treated them like extended family. One married couple worked there for thirty years, another for fourteen years. He was patient and steady. His time away from the farm was not spent only in church activities. He was good at keeping records and for a number of years he served as the secretary of the Knapdale School committee. When the much needed Otama water scheme was first established in the 1970s to serve farms in the Knapdale/Otama/Chatton areas, Clarence was one of the original committee members. He also loved to take time to talk to people, showing real interest in their lives. He was always forward looking. In his eighties he bought a hybrid car and installed solar water heating in the house. For as long as he was physically able, he helped his boys on their farms.

For years he regularly attended the annual Keswick Convention at Pounawea in the Catlins on the South Coast. From Boxing Day until New Year's Eve many families from throughout Southland and Otago would gather there. Accommodation was in dormitories on-site, or in privately owned caravans or local cribs. It was a unique opportunity to relax, to catch up with old friends or meet new ones, share meals together in the dining hall, help with vegetable preparation or dishes, and listen to inspiring Christian speakers. Children's programmes and free time in the afternoons created a family-friendly atmosphere.

Farming families enjoyed the short break in the midst of a busy summer season. So after Clarence married Margaret (nee Kerse) in 1957, they continued to attend. Their family of four children, Graeme, John, Helen and Jane, grew up knowing it was just what they did every summer. They have their own memories of those days.

Every convention featured a missions day, filled with challenging faith stories told by those who had returned or those who were about to leave to go overseas. Clarence had grown up with strong family links to missionaries and later he was part of Bible Class mission fundraising efforts. His lifelong interest came into full focus in 1989 when he and Margaret left New Zealand for their first overseas trip. Their destination was a SIM[1] field project in Ethiopia. Clarence wrote of his experiences during their five-week stay:

> My work was erecting the windmill and setting it up, laying piping to the storage tanks, and out to the compound for watering crops and trees. As it was the rainy season, there was a lot of draining to be done in the low-lying area and, being a Southlander, I felt at home on this job. The project had an aver-

1. SIM – Serving in Mission (formerly Sudan Interior Mission).

age of 240 workers who were paid 50 kilograms of wheat and two litres of cooking oil each fortnight.

It gave him first-hand understanding of conditions faced by missionaries in less developed countries. He had often heard others speak of similar challenges, but he also knew that it wasn't always physical factors which needed to be overcome.

Back in 1966 when Andrew and Margaret Dunn spoke on mission day at Pounawea, their plight certainly captured his attention. Here was a couple with two children, trained and ready to go to Papua New Guinea, but there was simply no funding available.

**Harry White** was at that same Pounawea Convention with his wife Margery and their young family of four boys: Rob, Malcolm, Richard and James. They were similar in age to the Gardyne children and, like the Gardynes, they went to Pounawea every year.

Harry had also left school at a young age, but that was due to ill health. He was in his late thirties when he married Margery Carter from Australia. He and his new bride settled in the Otama Homestead built in 1927 where he had grown up with his three sisters, one of whom had introduced him to Margery.

Harry and Clarence knew each other quite well. Their farms were only a fifteen minute drive apart and their respective churches were in neighbouring parishes.

In the mid-1960s, like his grandfather and father before him, Harry ran both cattle and sheep on his 1187-acre (480.3 ha) property. Over a period of time however, he decided the effort needed to maintain his Perendale/Romney sheep stud would be much better invested in beef cattle. Trading in cattle was his passion, his greatest skill and the source of his best returns. He had a great memory for stock, the price paid and the condition it was in at the time of purchase. He would buy poor and sell good. He could see the potential for the animals to grow out and believed in feeding them well. At one point the headcount of his cattle peaked at one thousand although that number was not sustained for long. As well as having an eye for trading in stock Harry was a good hand with a horse and he was an accomplished competitor at dog trials. At local events his heading and huntaway dogs performed well. In one competition he was placed sixth in the South Island. It was an outstanding achievement.

Margery was a great support to Harry. She was a woman who wasted nothing and who could live on the smell of an oily rag. The family used to joke that over the years she saved Harry thousands of dollars. She did not shirk hard work, but looking after her family of four boys kept her very busy. James had muscular dystrophy which required extra care, especially as he grew older and became less mobile. The boys were still at primary school in 1971 when Mary-Anne joined the family, chosen and adopted with love. The sheer pleasure and delight of having a daughter far outweighed the extra workload of having a baby in the house, while the boys doted on their new sister.

Coping with the huge amounts of washing, housework, baking and meals during those years required an extra pair of hands, provided by a succession of different housekeepers. When Elinor Collins arrived she quickly adapted, and a special bond grew between her and Mary-Anne. Their close-knit relationship has remained strong through the years, extending to include Mary-Anne's husband and family. During her time with the White family Elinor also became familiar with the Waidale Trust, little knowing that it would later become an integral part of her life.

In addition to a busy family and farm routines, Harry and Margery were a generous couple who offered warm hospitality and accommodation to dozens of people. Many visitors left with a car boot filled with meat, vegetables or eggs. Norman McIntosh was one of the many missionaries who developed close ties with the family. John Niven was also a regular visitor at the homestead. But he rarely came alone. He had a heart for the young people he worked with in Dunedin and would often bring a group down for a weekend, giving them an opportunity to be involved in a coffee bar outreach or other youth events. Sometimes the boys had to give up a bedroom for guests, or sleep wherever there was space. Many of those young people continue to be involved in pastoral work or mission today. It was a two-way street: missionaries and others were encouraged by the support they received from Harry and Margery, but they also left behind a positive lasting impression. The White boys saw evidence of a God who was real in the lives of their visitors; it was an example that consolidated the faith foundation laid by their parents.

The White home was also frequented for a number of years by international agricultural exchange students. Each girl would stay for a few months, helping mostly in the house but also on the farm. They loved the rural lifestyle. Farm workers merged with family and guests. Usually up to a dozen people would gather at the table for meals. Faith, culture and creed were not an issue. All were welcome.

Throughout those years, carving out time for farm chores and for people somehow fitted together. And then there were the annual sale days. Harry was a well-known figure at stock sales all round Southland, but he loved the chance to host a sale on his own property. For a number of years his focus was the Hereford heifer calves he had bought in the autumn. He would winter them over, put them to the bull in the spring and sell them the following March/April as in-calf heifers. He believed the stock would be in better condition if they were not transported to distant saleyards. Up to 500 animals would go under the auctioneer's hammer in a day, including some stock from neighbours who were glad of the opportunity to sell so close to home. His yards were down at the corner, very visible from the homestead. Elinor remembers those hectic days, preparing and serving morning and afternoon teas or lunch for all who attended.

John Speden, former stock agent and head auctioneer for Southland Farmers' Co-operative, had an excellent rapport with Harry. He can tell many stories: there was the time Harry was planning to purchase a block of land at Millers Flat. The property was being auctioned in Dunedin, and must have been scheduled for the afternoon, because when Harry hosted John for lunch at the Savoy, he offered him some advice:

'We've got to have fish, John.'

'Why is that Harry?'

'It's good for making brain cells work well.'

Harry won the auction and purchased the property. On another occasion when John was at the Otama homestead for dinner, someone commented on how good the beef tasted, whereupon Harry launched into a story of how the young heifer had suffered from bloat and needed to be put down. It was hardly dinner-time conversation, but that was Harry.

John had great respect for Harry, for his faith, for his farming skills and for his generosity. He saw him as a man who worked hard, who was genuine in both words and actions, but who could still laugh with you at the end of the day. Harry's association with John was the catalyst for the Waidale Trust making an annual donation to the local IHC branch, because he believed in their mission to 'advocate for the rights, inclusion and welfare of all people with intellectual disabilities and support them to live satisfying lives in the community.' John and his wife were involved with IHC because of their daughter and Waidale support for the organisation has continued through the years.

Harry was a very generous man. Once when floods wiped out of lot of fences, pasture and stock in the area, another stock agent –

who was also a farmer – thought he was buying lambs at a sale for Harry. But once the deal was completed, Harry turned to the agent and told him the stock was his to take home. Harry helped other farmers too in a similar way.

Harry's entrepreneurial skills enabled him to finance others into their own property. Bruce Heslip is just one person who owes a debt of gratitude to Harry. Bruce first worked for Harry in school holidays, or weekends, picking up wool in the woolshed at shearing time. When he was fifteen, Bruce was thinking of taking up a building apprenticeship, but the offer of a permanent, full-time position on the farm was too good to pass up. Harry was still single so it was no problem for Bruce to move into the homestead, sharing the house with married couple, Jack and Rona Hansen. Bruce remembers Harry singing quite a lot around the house, but the one image that has always remained with him always is seeing him kneeling, praying by his bed in the evening.

Harry was ahead of his time in many ways. His sons Rob and Richard recall that he was always thinking of better ways to do things. They recall him experimenting with drenching the sheep using a mixture of Maxicrop and vinegar. The boys would be most annoyed if the mixture blocked the guns, or caused the sheep to cough and splutter. Harry even tried making silage out of thistles.

They also remember when Harry established the practice of shifting cattle daily between feed breaks. Much later it was demonstrated as a new technique at a rural field day. A neighbour who attended the field day was bemused at how this 'new' practice was being promoted when in fact it was something Harry had used twenty years before.

The Whites crammed a lot of life into each week: as well as farming, there was also church. All work on the farm ceased on Sunday, except for essential stock work such as lambing. Harry was an elder in the Riversdale/Waikaia/Wendon parish. Every Sunday the family piled into their car and drove over the hill to the little church at Wendon. Harry helped with Sunday school there and also with youth group at Riversdale. On a Friday night, in the days before seatbelts, he would make the fifteen minute drive in the family car crammed full of young people. He never wavered in his weekly commitment even when he was in his fifties.

Life for the White family fitted around their parents' activities and, although they saw his flaws, his sons remember their dad as faithful and dedicated, a man who loved God and whose very real faith was shown in the most practical ways. Many a carcass was cut up, packed and donated to individuals or organisations like Youth for Christ. He grew three paddocks of Timothy-grass seed that was sold to raise funds for the church, or donated to others for their fundraising. It was a bit of a process cutting, binding and stooking the grass, and putting it through his threshing mill. The seed wasn't just a handout either, because the recipients still had to find buyers. If Harry knew a person with a genuine need for finance or a vehicle, he would offer to help in whatever way was appropriate.

He believed that you had to have a reason for making money. Richard summed up his dad's attitude: 'If it wasn't for the giving side of it, Dad couldn't see much point in farming.'

At Pounawea, when Harry and Clarence first discussed raising money to support the Dunns, it was a cause they were both keen to support.

They could not have imagined how the idea would explode to become something much bigger. But their first step was to approach Andrew and Margaret.

**Andrew and Margaret Dunn.** Andrew clearly remembers the discussion with Harry and Clarence that Sunday afternoon. He describes it as 'one of those electric moments'.

Andrew and Margaret (nee Parsons) first met at Easter in

Dunedin at a Christian Endeavour (CE) camp.[2] It was Andrew's younger sister Aynsley who introduced them. Margaret was her good friend and prior to the camp she had invited her home for a couple of days. Andrew's father was very impressed with Margaret, thought she would make a great match for Andrew and wasted no time in writing to tell him so. Andrew's interest was further ignited when he heard her parents saying publicly at the CE camp that they were willing for their children to be involved in mission.

Margaret didn't need to be coerced because she was already thinking seriously about mission and with that goal in mind she graduated from Otago University with a BA followed by teacher training in Christchurch. While in Dunedin she attended the Evangelical Union, where visiting speakers captured her attention and her interest in mission grew, especially in the work of the Bolivian Indian Mission (BIM). As she and Andrew came to know each other a little better, she learnt that his parents had also considered going to Bolivia, but the outbreak of the Second World War prevented them taking the matter further.

Andrew enjoyed a happy childhood with his three sisters at their home, Knowtop, on the top of the Broughton Street hill in Gore. There was plenty of room to play on their two-acre lifestyle block that was also home to two cows, a pig, some hens and a horse. The family never had to buy milk, butter or eggs from the grocer. Warm hospitality was a hallmark of the Dunn home. His parents, Cliff and Edith, often welcomed extended family, friends and other visitors for meals and for missionary meetings. Andrew was deeply impressed by the mission stories he heard and the regular 'magic

---

2. Christian Endeavour was a very popular interdenominational youth organisation which encouraged its members to be diligent and committed to their church, to read the Bible and pray, and to engage in mission. From its beginnings in America it spread widely, reaching New Zealand in the early twentieth century.

lantern' slide evenings. Cliff supported his family by working as a clerk for stock and station agent Wright Stephenson until he was called up for army service. On his return home he joined his brother at the Waimumu lime works but he was looking for a change of direction. His application for Presbyterian ministry training was accepted; it was a scheme for returned servicemen. Andrew recalls:

> So we left Gore in April 1947 for Kowai Parish in North Canterbury where Dad worked for seven years, five as a home missionary while he studied on the job, and then two more as a fully ordained minister. From there he moved to Morven in South Canterbury and later to Owaka on the south coast.

The years at Morven were tinged with sadness, for it was there that Andrew's mother Edith died of cancer. It was also a time of change for him. He finished school having gained School Certificate, and moved to Christchurch to train with Civil Aviation at the RNZAF operational base at Wigram. He enjoyed his work in radio communications and was well on his way to gaining his pilot's licence when he went home in 1958 for the Christmas holidays. His father had remarried and with his new wife Anne was now based at the Owaka Parish in the Catlins, only a few minutes' drive from Pounawea. John Deane was one of the main speakers at the Convention that year. He was the Principal of the Bible Training Institute (BTI) in Auckland.[3] So when Cliff Dunn invited John and his wife to share a meal at the manse, it was a great opportunity to renew friendships. For Andrew, however, it was the lunch date that changed everything.

John was keen to hear how Andrew was doing. It wasn't that

3. BTI was later known as the Bible College of New Zealand and is currently known as Laidlaw College.

they were strangers. They had kept in touch intermittently since a Keswick Convention at Motukarara in Canterbury a couple of years before when Andrew had made the significant decision to make himself available for mission should God lead him in that direction. Now John listened as he spoke enthusiastically of his plans. He was certain that his civil aviation training would stand him in good stead for mission in the years ahead. It seemed a logical choice. Papua New Guinea was one of the key areas where Presbyterian missionaries were working and aircraft were widely used there for transport. He was, however, quite unprepared for the older man's response and his blunt advice:

> We don't need more pioneers or pilots in Papua New Guinea. What they need there are theologically trained people who can help shape the future of the church for the next generation. Get back into short pants and go and get your University Entrance. Then go on to Otago University and to Knox College and get a theological degree.

Andrew was stunned. He felt as if he had run into a brick wall.

> My friend and I were tenting on the lawn at the manse because the house was full. I remember for two or three days I was on my knees for hours out in that tent by the rhododendron bush pestering with this thing. And finally the Lord came through, and I had a sense of 'Wow, this is astonishing. I would never have dreamed of this. Maybe I am up to it.'

Once he had made up his mind, he felt strangely peaceful and as he began to pursue his change of direction, things fell into place.

> I discovered that at Otago you could get into university

> under provisional matriculation when you were 21 years old. I couldn't get in that year, because I wasn't yet of age. So I resigned from Civil Aviation, worked on my cousin's farm for a year up at Clydevale in the Clutha Valley, and applied through the Presbytery. Their student committee and the new Clutha Valley parish minister were all very enthusiastic and supportive of the idea. I applied, I was accepted and I began at University in 1960.

During the months since Andrew and Margaret had first met in Dunedin they continued to correspond by letter and, after he had moved there to commence his study, their relationship grew. Their engagement was followed by marriage in 1962, when Andrew was in his third year as a divinity student. He graduated with a BA and a BD. At the Pounawea Convention in 1966 they were introduced with their two young daughters, Karen and Lynette. Two months later Andrew was ordained and inducted for missionary service at the Otama church, which was part of the Knapdale-Waikaka Parish. It was a privilege for his father, who was ministering in the parish, to present Andrew formally on this significant occasion.

Although Andrew and Margaret's application to serve in Papua New Guinea had been accepted by the Presbyterian Overseas Missions Committee, until funding became available they could not make any travel plans. While they waited they filled an interim vacancy in the Tokanui Parish, which was also in the Catlins, but closer to Invercargill.

***

### Establishment of The Waidale Trust

After the Pounawea Convention, Harry and Clarence took the

idea of raising support for the Dunns back to their fellow session members in their respective parishes. Clarence introduced it at Knapdale-Waikaka. Harry made a similar approach at Riversdale-Waikaia. Both sessions responded positively and appointed representatives to establish a committee. Bert Gardyne, George Simpson, Harry White and Ron Paterson were entrusted with the task. They met three times before convening a public meeting at the Otama Presbyterian church on 5 June 1967, where Andrew and Margaret came and shared their story. Veteran missionary, Norman McIntosh, spoke at that meeting in support of the Dunns, comparing the building of the church in Papua New Guinea with David's desire to build the temple.

The decision was made to form the Waidale Missionary Fellowship with the purpose of financing, encouraging and prayerfully supporting Andrew and Margaret Dunn. But the vision didn't stop there. Rather, they looked ahead, agreeing to promote missionary interest and support other avenues of service in the future.

The elected committee consisted of Ron Paterson (Chairman), George Simpson (Secretary), Harry White (Treasurer), Stan Clark, Pamela Davies, Bert Gardyne, Clarence Gardyne, Pearson Johnston, Lewis Mackay, Don Tayles, Margery White and Bruce Wilson.

The idea of creating a charitable trust prompted further discussion which enlarged their vision. A trust would be an effective and viable way to protect and grow financial assets, thus increasing the potential for donating funds. All those involved agreed it was the best way forward. Once the decision was made the process began and less than three months later, on 28 August 1967, The Waidale Missionary Trust was ratified and formalised.

The name 'Waidale' is a combination of the names of the two contributing parishes – Waikaka and Riversdale. In the Maori language *wai* means water, while the word *dale* is an old English word meaning valley. The images are most appropriate for mission and can be linked to many Bible verses which relate to Jesus offering the water of life and the abundant blessings which result from that.

Trading and grazing stock would be the main form of income while donations, interest-bearing and interest-free loans and bank overdraft facilities provided an excellent financial base. Harry White, who had also been appointed stock supervisor, wasted no time in making purchases of stock on behalf of the Trust, and facilitating their distribution to graziers. Harry was familiar with how to operate a successful trust, as more than ten years previously he had established the Otama Trust as a means to donate money to worthwhile causes, mostly Christian mission. Many who had committed to contributing to the Waidale Trust were on large farms that had been passed down through the generations. But Harry knew that size did not matter. One farmer faithfully donated 100 lambs each year. It was a significant donation from a small 200-acre (80.9 ha) block that had been allocated as part of the rehabilitation scheme for returned soldiers.

**There is no one who is insignificant in the purpose of God.**
- Alistair Begg

As support for Waidale grew, those who were not farmers found other ways to contribute. Some preferred to make a cash donation, while two other families focused on honey and hens.

For a number of years, beekeeper Jim Simpson set aside 20 hives for Waidale. Once expenses had been deducted, all profits from the honey sales from those beehives were donated to Waidale.

Meanwhile Andrew's father, Cliff, saw potential in raising money for Waidale through selling eggs. Peter Dunn recalls the venture when they lived in the old manse at Waikaka, located just up the road from the church:

> Dad bought, or was given, a set of wire battery cages for 24 hens from the local egg farm in Waikaka. He also got the hens

from there which were replaced every year. I can remember the old ones being dispatched, plucked and gutted and put into the freezer, scrawny as they were. After the manure was cleaned out and put onto the garden, there was the excitement of the new hens arriving. We had a 44 gallon drum of mash which we mixed with warm water at feed time. We kids also made sure the water supply to the hens was full all the time and we had a sack of crushed oyster shell for the hens. When they were laying we collected the eggs before and after school. They were washed and dried and put into brown paper bags in half dozen and dozen lots and stored in the shed under the water tank. They were sold to locals and I can remember seeing them in Kelly's Four Square shop in Waikaka as well.

In the early days of the Trust, another farmer planted Douglas firs suitable for milling for the timber industry. Such an investment requires little upkeep, and now, nearly fifty years on, is expected to bring an excellent return.

**Mission assignment begins.** After the establishment of the Waidale Trust, it took less than a year to make $4,500 available to cover all of the Dunn's expenses at the All Saints College in Sydney. They needed to spend six months in orientation there to prepare for the vastly different culture they would encounter in Papua New Guinea. Finally their appointment to the Papua Mainland Synod of the United Church in Papua New Guinea and the Solomon Islands was confirmed. Their farewell by the Mataura Presbytery at Waikaka on 28 November 1967 was followed three weeks later by a function at the Wendon church where friends and supporters of Waidale gathered to say goodbye. It was a defining moment, both for the members of the Waidale Trust and for the Dunn family.

Their time in Sydney proved to be a valuable blend of learning practical skills, missiology, Bible teaching and essential medical practices. Understanding the way in which Australia was administering PNG was also important. Lectures and classes were shared between the missionary training college, the Australian School of Pacific Administration and the School of Tropical Medicine. This type of specialised training was not available in New Zealand. Andrew spent two weeks learning about outboard motors at an Outboard Marine factory. Moving from a country where motor vehicles are the most common form of transport, to the Purari Delta area meant a huge change of thinking. Boats, not wheels, would now carry them everywhere.

By the time they flew to Port Moresby in July 1968, baby Stephen had joined their family. A warm welcome from Betty and Albert Scarlet to their home at Saroa, about an hour's drive from Port Moresby, gave them their first taste of a new country, a new language and a new culture. The days that followed were a whirlwind of information and introductions. Albert was able to give Andrew an overview of the United Church's district work and administrative systems which he would be responsible for managing. The family spent a few nights at the Ruatoka Teachers' College, also run by the church, and met with some of the students and staff. They returned to the United Church headquarters at Metoreia, near Port Moresby, where they met other church leaders including Bishop Ravu Henao who took them under his wing. They began to understand more of their new responsibilities. It would be a huge undertaking and they also needed to begin learning the Hiri Motu lingua franca, one of seven hundred languages used in the country. A month soon passed before they flew out to the Delta, 150 miles northwest of Moresby. A Missionary Aviation Fellowship Cessna flew them to Kikori to participate in a Delta Schools Music Festival at Aird Hill School where they met with the mission education leaders, teachers and pupils before going on to Kapuna, their home for the next six years.

They spent a month with John and Hazel Cribb who were retiring. Andrew was to succeed John as Superintendent Minister for the Delta Circuit. There was a lot to learn about the job and how to live and thrive in the isolation and beauty of the tropical rain forest. Andrew recalls their first impressions:

> There wasn't a walking track anywhere. We walked down from our house steps and onto the jetty. Our church district actually spanned 70-80 miles of river delta country; the rivers came down from the Highlands and fanned out into this amazing network.

He remembered what John Deane had said and realised the truth of his words, that the church in PNG did not need pioneers, but rather trained people. Nevertheless he felt very much like a rookie in this new environment where he was not only a pastor, but also an accountant, business manager and head missionary. He was responsible for seventy people, including pastoral staff throughout the area, teachers from Australia, the United Kingdom and Papua New Guinea, medical orderlies in village posts, an Australian who ran the outboard maintenance workshop and a Samoan couple who managed the copra plantation. It was almost overwhelming but, because they saw God at every step of their journey, they knew they were not alone, and they did not feel daunted. Andrew reflects:

> It was incredible that the strands all came together. The idea of Waidale was just sitting there. Harry had established the Otama Trust and various people, including some of his farming friends like Lewis Mackay were helping to manage it. Our need came along, but all of this was unknown to them and it just so happened that we all ended up at Keswick together that Christmas where I was invited to tell my story. Without Waidale support

> the finance would have been raised eventually, I am sure, but it would have been too late for the appointment in PNG. So it was God's timing for everything.

Andrew's job involved not only managing the Delta Circuit of the United Church but also ushering in a new phase of development. The church, which had been established sixty years before by the London Missionary Society, was growing and functioning so well it had reached a stage where it was time to prepare for nationals to step into leadership roles. But it wouldn't happen overnight. Careful management of the existing work and the widespread geographical area of the church meant Andrew was often away, leaving Margaret at home base. She was by no means alone as she looked after their three children, worked with staff wives and participated in local Kapuna Church activities. Next door was Kapuna Hospital[4] where doctors Lin and Peter Calvert headed up an excellent team training nursing staff and medical orderlies to a level where they were capable of running medical clinics in the villages. Lin and Peter continually worked to adapt modern medicine in a way that could be applied by locals in their villages.

Margaret's teacher training was put to good use as each of their children turned five. Their home became a classroom and the Correspondence School in New Zealand provided materials and support. When their daughter Cathy was born at home, with support from the hospital staff, they were delighted with the new addition to their family. However, as she grew Andrew and Margaret noticed her delayed speech and physical development; Cathy was examined and diagnosed with cerebral palsy. Overcoming the challenges that brought was difficult but not insurmountable. When it was time for more formal learning, Margaret liaised with The

4. www.kapuna.org

Correspondence School that sent equipment and a specially designed programme for Cathy. Her early setback did not prevent her achieving and today she holds two university degrees.

Being a missionary certainly does not insulate you from life's difficulties, and in 1973 the Dunn family was tested a second time. They were expecting another addition to their family but sadly their baby son Robert did not survive his premature birth, despite professional medical care from Lin Calvert and her best efforts to save him. Margaret, who also nearly lost her life, owes a debt of gratitude to Peter Calvert whose superb intervention brought her through those days. Throughout this time of deep grief, sadness and loss, their faith remained strong but their understanding of the cost of their call to mission and ministry was severely tested. Such crises in life can raise many questions as to why obedience to God's call should bring with it such a cost. Robert's death also impacted the local people. Andrew reflects:

> They saw that we suffered too, just as they did. We were no longer above the human issues of life in the swamp and heat and rain and mozzies.

It took some weeks for Margaret to recover, which meant extra responsibility for Andrew who helped care for their children. Even with great support from other people it was still a very difficult time. Robert has never been forgotten, and as recently as November 2017, Jennifer Koelet from New Zealand, who teaches at Kapuna School, sent the family a photo of the gravesite which had been cleared and decorated with flowers by the school children there. Andrew remembers the difficulty of having to craft a headstone in a place where there was no gravel or stones, so he improvised using river sand and broken outboard motor parts. The inscription reads *Ekalesia Helaro Toreisi Lou* meaning 'The hope of the church is the resurrection.' The support of those at home was invaluable, especially during these times. Andrew and Margaret visited New Zealand every three years, which gave them an opportunity to catch up with family, visit those who supported them and to take a much-needed break from the pressures of living in a culture that was so different.

Growth and change always go together. In those first years financial support for the Dunn family came entirely from the Waidale Trust. But Waidale gave so much more than money. They supplied valuable partnership on several levels. Trust members were invested in this family. They wrote letters, they prayed, and they were keen to read the newsletters which arrived by snail mail. Sometimes Andrew would send sets of coloured slides and an audio tape commentary, which were widely circulated among members, prayer groups and families. When the Dunn family arrived home on furlough, their itinerary always included a visit to catch up with Trust members and supporters.

Then, after nearly six years of being based in Kapuna, Andrew was asked to consider filling a pastoral vacancy at the Ela-Boroko United Church of Papua New Guinea in Port Moresby. It was a significant change in direction. The time the family had spent in the delta area had been an amazing adventure during which they had grown in their faith and as people, but it had also taken its toll on their family. The time seemed right for this move and, although relocating to the capital would bring new challenges, it would be a great bonus to be living in a city. Andrew and Margaret accepted the call, which gave Andrew overall responsibility for three congregations. Support would now come from the local church, so the need for finances from Waidale ceased, but the links which had been forged with members of the Trust and the local Eastern Southland parishes was to remain strong over the coming years.

### A snapshot of mission in history

When the Dunn family first moved to Port Moresby, the Ela-Boroko congregations included leading Papua New Guinean heads of government departments, university staff from around the world, public servants, teachers, doctors, nurses and workers in many trades. Andrew was responsible not only for the church but also for chairing the board of the United Church building, a six-storey building investment in the centre of the Port Moresby CBD which housed an embassy, the head offices of some large national businesses as well as church offices and leaders. The funds generated were used to support various programmes, mission and community initiatives.

At the same time independence was looming for the nation which created diverse feelings and reactions among the nationals. As the time drew closer, many people began to feel vulnerable and uncertain which led to a deep need for God and His grace. Some felt that independence was coming too soon, while for others it couldn't come soon enough. In the Boroko suburb alone, all the churches – Anglicans, Baptists, Catholics, United and others – reflected this concern and grew as a result.

As Andrew began to open the word of God in his congregations they began to grow. The 10am Boroko congregation doubled in size every two years. The church would be full and many more would be sitting outside on the lawn. After the Dunns returned home in 1979, it was decided to build a new church down the road. In later years, when Andrew and daughter Cathy returned on a visit, folk were apologising to them because only 1,200 turned up that Sunday in the church built to hold 2,000 people. A different sort of revival happened out in the Delta. It was more charismatic with signs and wonders, whereas in Port Moresby it was more of a hunger and thirst to understand the things of God.

Papua New Guinea became self-governing in 1973 and achieved independence on 16 September 1975. On the day of celebration the Dunn family joined thousands of others in the big stadium in Port Moresby. As the Australian flag came down, they noticed some people around them crying, saying it was too soon, while others celebrated joyfully. Andrew looks back and sees that the gospel had a huge role to play, which is reflected in a statement in the new constitution: 'We are a Christian country.'

The Presbyterian Church no longer has missionaries in PNG. The church there is almost entirely indigenous.

**Waidale continues to move forward.** With the Dunn family now being supported by their church, the reason the Waidale Trust was established no longer existed. However, there were plenty of other missions and missionaries who needed support. Each application was given due consideration and no decision was reached without much prayer and discussion.

Harry and Margery hosted most of the Trust meetings at their Otama homestead. Rob and Richard remember the buzz as people arrived because they had a clear view up the passage from their bedrooms. For the Trust members, some of whom farmed in quite isolated locations, there was the added bonus of the opportunity to have a good yarn with other farmers. Without doubt those meetings nurtured *koinonia*, a Greek word that can be loosely defined as family, home, or meeting together with a common goal and fellowship.

Not all the work of the Trust occurred at meetings. Less than a year after their formation, in June 1968, they hosted a missionary exhibition in the Waikaka Centennial Hall. The Dunn family and their work in Papua was the central focus of their display. The following year, when another exhibition was held at Merino Downs, they created a similar presentation.

The blueprint and reason for Waidale's existence, to support mission, remained constant. However, rather like a kaleidoscope, the colours and the pattern kept evolving. As personal commitments changed, some of the original thirteen trustees resigned but others took their place. By the tenth anniversary the total number of trustees had not changed but there were some different faces at the meetings.

**George Simpson and Jim McNamara.** After seven years, Secretary George Simpson decided to step down. It was a time-consuming role and he was a single man who had a farm to run as well as keeping himself at home. But he remained a Trust member for a further forty years.

A minute of appreciation was recorded for his very capable service:

> George, having been secretary since the formation of the Trust, has played a large part in forming and laying the foundation. His efficiency, enthusiasm and wise counsel, coupled with his

> deep commitment to our Lord are an inspiration to us all. We value very much his continuing service as a Trustee.

Jim McNamara replaced George as secretary and served for seven years until he and his wife Janice left for Australia. During that time Jim's passion for the Trust included many voluntary hours of transporting stock. His enthusiasm for Waidale has remained vibrant, reflected in his greeting at the time of the 50th Jubilee:

> From the beginning the Waidale Missionary Trust has been an encouragement and an inspiration to Janice and me because out of a need God gave a vision and when faithful men and women responded he blessed it abundantly. What an amazing journey. What a testimony to the blessings poured out from the hand of God … many of those who were involved from the start are still active for His Kingdom. What an example.

***

## Other Missionaries Supported in the Early Years

**Dave and Lynette Salisbury.** Waidale supported Dave Salisbury of Open Air Campaigners who, with his wife Lynette, moved to Zambia in 1973 to begin an evangelism programme. Twenty-five years later Suzette McNamara (Jim's daughter) went with seven other young people on a short-term mission trip to Zambia where they worked with Dave and Lynette. The trip impacted their lives in a significant way and all of them continued in full-time Christian ministry in later years. Jim and Janice have also travelled to Zambia several times. Exciting opportunities for sharing the gospel there have expanded their vision for mission.

**Chris and Helen Cowie.** About the same time as the Salisburys went to Zambia, Chris Cowie and his wife Helen were accepted by SIM. For more than forty years they served in Benin and Niger in West Africa. Later they were the SIM New Zealand mission directors. Chris reflects:

> Each year, the Waidale Trust generously contributed to our support that enabled us to continue in our ministries. They never wavered in meeting their regular support contributions. We could count on it even when the farming economy was going through hard times. For us this was the miracle! A big thank you to the members of the Waidale Trust for their faithfulness and working so hard towards this.
>
> During my time of leadership of SIM NZ, I was so thankful to the Trust in another way. At times I had either new missionary candidates or missionaries wanting to return to their country of ministry who were lacking support and just couldn't raise additional support. On some occasions I shared these specific needs with Waidale leadership and often the invitation would be received for the missionaries concerned to come and share with Trust members. This was a tremendous help and God often used this opportunity to make it possible for missionaries to commence or return to their ministry countries. Again, a big thank you to the Waidale Trust for their generous faith in contributing to additional requests.
>
> I love the way the Waidale Trust is continuing and how the original vision is being grasped by another generation. Helen and I feel very privileged and blessed for the long-term association we have had with the great people of Waidale. Our sincere thanks for the way each member has responded to God's calling on their lives.

**Margaret Currie (nee Wyber).** Margaret Wyber loved reading. So when a school friend gave her a book as a birthday gift, she was soon absorbed in the life of Annie James[5] who went as a missionary to China in 1912. Annie's story planted a dream in Margaret's heart. One day she wanted to go to China too.

Margaret's personal faith journey began when school friends, who were from Christian families, invited her to stay for a weekend. For Margaret the highlight of those visits was going to Sunday school. When she was a little older, some of those friends invited her to go with them to the Pounawea Convention, where she became a Christian and heard other mission stories.

Marge McLeod, a friend she met during her nursing training at Balclutha hospital, became the person God used to lead her to Mongolia. But first, before Waidale had even been established, Margaret went to Malaysia, with the Overseas Missionary Fellowship (OMF), where she spent ten years working in Borneo and Sarawak. Some of her students wanted to attend Christian youth camps, but could not afford the fees, so she was both encouraged and relieved to begin to receive funding from Waidale. There were many testimonies from the young people at the camps, who discovered God to be real, as He empowered them to grow in their Christian lives. When Margaret's visa was cancelled by the Malaysian government in 1976 and she was ordered out of Sarawak, she returned to New Zealand but yet never lost hope that one day she would go to China. She thought this might be her opportunity.

Instead an unexpected romance unfolded when she met and married widower Len Currie in Gore. Eleven years later she was widowed and believed the time was now right to fulfil her childhood dream of going to China to teach English. She began to work

---

5. Snowden, R. F. (1948). *Never a dull moment: Life and letters of Annie James*. Dunedin: Presbyterian Bookroom.

with OMF towards that goal, and was excited about the prospect. Her initial preparation was interrupted when Marge returned home from Mongolia because of a serious illness. Margaret went to help her friend and to nurse her back to health. During her recuperation Marge was constantly talking about returning to Mongolia. Her zeal impressed Margaret. One day Marge told Margaret that 100 young people from China were going into Mongolia to teach English. For Margaret it changed everything. Her immediate response was, 'I'd rather go and teach English myself.' She knew that Mongolia had been under Chinese rule for 800 years and guessed it was likely that the Chinese tutors would be simply a cover for the spread of communism.

So Margaret changed her plans, applied to Waidale for support, and in 1992 flew with Marge to the capital Ulaanbaatar. For three years she taught English there. Everything changed again when one of her students wanted to visit her brother in prison. Margaret went along to support her. She was appalled at the conditions inside: basic human rights were non-existent; many of the inmates had been given harsh sentences – some for life; others were on death row, while still others were serving a disproportionate amount of time for menial, petty crimes. She saw an opportunity to make a difference. It was not easy and she often worked in difficult conditions, assessing needs, keeping contact with families who may well have been ostracised by the community and advocating with the authorities on behalf of the prisoners. It required lots of patient perseverance working among the inmates of 23 prisons and 20 detention centres. Many prisoners were dying every day as a result of illness and depression. At first it seemed an impossible task. But nothing is ever impossible with God. Help came from an unexpected quarter

**We are all faced with a series of great opportunities brilliantly disguised as impossible situations.**
– Chuck Swindoll

– one very worried senior prison official. His colleague, a general in Russia, advised him to set up Prison Fellowship International, a Christian humanitarian aid organisation for prisoners and their families. He was an atheistic communist but he was desperate and willing to try anything. His colleague gave a positive report because it was working well in Russia. He advised him to call the international headquarters of Prison Fellowship in Washington and ask for help. When the representative arrived from Washington, the senior official sent him to see Margaret.

For twenty-four years Margaret continued the work, showing Christ's love to the men and their families. She endured many hardships in a country where temperatures soar to 40 degrees celsius in summer and plummet to minus 40 in winter. She participated in community life, including membership of the BayanZurkh Rotary Club, where she served as president for two years and was made a Paul Harris Fellow.

Mongolians love to celebrate public occasions with pomp and ceremony and they certainly celebrated when the Mongolian Ministry of Justice awarded Margaret an order of merit to acknowledge her work. The last thing she ever wanted was public recognition but God used it to open new doors for support and to provide more finance for the work in the prisons. She has also been made a Member of the New Zealand Order of Merit, and Prison Fellowship has presented her with the Elizabeth Fry award, conferred to:

> recognise her as a person whose life exhibits a deep love for God and love for prisoners, whose courage and persistence in caring for prisoners is an inspiration to many; whose life and witness has mobilised Christian compassion and action in bringing dignity and hope to prisoners.

Margaret didn't ever want any awards. In her own words: 'Missionaries don't look for medals. I just want to hear Jesus say, "Well done. Now you can go and sit down."'

***

## Waidale and Three Generations of One Family

During the first decade there were many people who were God's giants, yet their hallmark was humility of spirit. Norman McIntosh was one of those people. He was held in high regard by members and supporters of the Trust; like them, his life was a living example of dreaming big.

Waidale has supported three generations of the McIntosh family: Norman and Amy; daughter Averil and Alan Bennett, and son Gavin and Jenny McIntosh; and granddaughter Kristina and John Tipper. However, the relationship has not been one-sided, it has been a mutual partnership.

**Norman and Amy McIntosh.** Norman was born into a Southland farming family near Wyndham. But, when only five years old, he faced the double calamity of his mother's death and, not long afterwards, their house burnt to the ground. His father moved the family to the Geraldine area in South Canterbury to seek work, and eventually he remarried. Norman's stepmother brought stability, love and kindness into their home. But times were hard and there was little money. Norman had to shoulder responsibility beyond his years. His life was shaped by long days and hard work, both at school and at home. Although his own mother had been a woman of faith and prayer, there was no other Christian influence in their home after her death. But that changed when Mr Bob Morrison, a Brethren businessman in Geraldine, asked Norman's father if he would send the children to Sunday school at Woodbury. For Norman it was the beginning of a journey towards God. As a teenager he struggled for some years with God's persistent voice, calling him to admit he was a sinner and to accept the free gift of salvation. Finally one night, after casually slipping into a hall in town, he heard Mr Alex Mill of the Egypt General Mission speaking and Norman knew he could ignore God's voice no longer. He rode his horse back to the lonely shepherd's hut where he was living and working, found the Bible packed in his trunk and threw it on his bed where it happened to open at Romans chapter five. He accepted Christ as his Saviour and a great miracle occurred:

> He declared later he had also had the sense of taking himself in his hands, as it were, and offering himself to God for service, totally, unconditionally and forever. The battle was over. The simple shepherd's hut seemed full of the glory of the Lord.[6]

Over the following months he attended Bible studies in Geraldine, but he also met other Christian young people from the Ashburton Baptist Church where he was baptised some time later. One of the girls from youth group gave him a copy of the Baptist magazine and the only thing he remembered reading in it was an advertisement for the Bible Training Institute in Auckland. He knew nothing about it but felt God prompted him to apply. His application was rejected but he was so certain God wanted him there he wrote and appealed their decision and was overjoyed to be accepted. He was excited but nervous because he had not grown up in a church and was not sure what to expect. Yet, before he graduated in 1935, he knew God had called him to China. While at

---

6. Hinton, L. (1987). *Never say can't.* Singapore: Overseas Missionary Fellowship (IHQ) Ltd.

BTI he met Amy Carter, another candidate with the China Inland Mission. She was single-minded about her call and reluctant to respond to any romantic notions. However, when her departure was delayed, an unexpected window of opportunity opened for the two of them to become better acquainted. During their courtship they often discussed their faith and their call. Their experiences had taught them that nothing was impossible with God. Shortly before they became engaged the two of them sincerely agreed that, as far as obedience to God was concerned, the word 'can't' would be struck out of their vocabulary. They were blessed with six children, yet that did not stop them being obedient to God's call to serve overseas.

After sixteen years as pioneer missionaries in China with OMF they were deported in 1952 by the Communist regime. They also served God in Tibet, Malaya, Indonesia and the Philippines. When Waidale Trust was established they supported it wholeheartedly and the Trust also supported them. Their daughter Averil recalls:

> I often went with Dad on deputation trips to draughty church halls around Gore, where I helped show the slides and revelled in his delight at sharing God's miraculous interventions along the Tibetan border. After one such a visit he packed up and left only to be chased down the road by Harry White and brought back to talk further. Among the dynamic people of Waidale Dad experienced the richness of a spiritual family. Most of them were farmers who took time off at Easter and Labour weekends to support Pukerau Bible Class camp, now Camp Columba, and the New Year week at Pounawea Keswick Convention. It was there that Norman McIntosh and other missionaries returned to share their vision for God's world.

**If God is your partner, make your plans BIG.**
– DL Moody

Norman's early years taught him an indelible lesson: embrace Father God's vision for the world then hurdle all the impossibilities by prayerful, canny problem-solving and a skilful pair of hands. Averil remembers him telling her, 'Dream big, Ave! And don't despise the little things. Little victories become big ones.'

**Alan and Averil Bennett.** After graduating from Gore High School, Averil stayed in a hall of residence at Otago University in Dunedin where she shared a room with Margaret Parsons (Dunn). The college warden designated the rooms, but the two young women believed God had placed them together. Little did they know the way in which Waidale would become a common thread in both of their lives. They shared their aspirations as teachers, they were both involved with Evangelical Union (EU) – later called the Christian Union – and their shared mission focus was confirmed by Dr Masumi Toyotome whose catch cry, 'Asia for Christ in our generation', initiated a mission revival.

Averil reflects on the impact of the Waidale Trust on the lives of their family:

> From the very beginning, Waidale's commitment went beyond a financial one. The members became prayer companions. They stored decrepit furniture in a farm barn during the long years between furloughs and gave us great times on the farm during them. While our parents were in Southeast Asia, they sent farm produce up to us four young McIntoshes at university. Their love then extended to our own children while we were in Thailand: they arranged for summer jobs and board. One even baked and decorated a surprise twenty-first birthday cake! Later, our son was so deeply affected by James White's courageous approach to life with muscular dystrophy, that he studied biochemistry at Otago and now researches inflammatory diseases.

Alan and I were supported by gifts from Waidale for most of the forty-two years we were church planting with OMF and FEBC[7] in Thailand.

Alan was the field leader for OMF in Central Thailand during, and in the aftermath of the Vietnam War. It was a time of high stress for missionaries with pressure to contain and retrench. Every spiritual advance met with vicious opposition. One fellow worker was shot while leading a home group, another beaten up. We were all burgled. In Thailand in 1978 my sister Twink and her children died in a horrific road accident, which also killed two missionary surgeons with their entire families. It severely tested the ministry of Manorom Christian Hospital; Twink's husband, Bryan Parry, was suddenly the only surgeon left.[8] Waidale's gifts supported Manorom's hospital and leprosy work. It is estimated that 50% of Christians in Central Thailand came to know Christ through the medical programme.

Each gift from the Waidale Trust came with a news-filled annual letter from the secretary. Letter writing was a special and much-appreciated ministry of the wives of Waidale men. When Elinor Collins became secretary she wrote so informatively we could visualise how God was blessing Waidale. Letters arrived at just the right time to encourage us even though mail delivery was spasmodic.

Their spirits were lifted even more when Harry White and Norman McIntosh travelled together in 1981 to visit Alan and

7. FEBC (Far East Broadcasting Company) is an interdenominational ministry whose sole purpose is to share the Good News to the world through radio, the Internet, and emerging technologies.

8. Gordon-Smith, I. (1981) *In his time*. Compiled by E.L. Gordon-Smith. Leeds, UK: Stanley L. Hunt (Printers) Ltd.

Averil in Thailand. Harry encouraged them, and the team at Manorom Hospital, to expand their vision and urged them to trust God for a harvest, despite the circumstances. His fragile health scared them and he was exhausted after each busy, humid day. Yet it did not dampen his enthusiasm, or motivation. He would race home, strip off his 'respectable' clothing, and sprawl in shorts and bare feet. Laughter, which had been scarce, returned.

**Kristina and John Tipper.**

> Waidale support has made a significant difference, both financially and prayerfully, to our ministry with Operation Mercy among the displaced. Waidale financial support comes to us annually in a lump sum. Because we have to pay our rent annually, the provision of that money is always timely and it is wonderful to know we don't have to worry where the rent money is coming from. We are encouraged when people visit us. We were delighted to welcome Margaret Gardyne's grandson, Liam, who visited us in 2017 during his gap year.
>
> When we come home to New Zealand on leave, meeting people who have prayed into specific situations of need is also a great blessing.

**Tenth Anniversary**
**9 July 1977**

Venue: Otama Hall

During the shared tea meal there were several speakers:

- Harry White outlined the formation and history of the Waidale Trust
- Janet Harrington (WEC)
- Gordon Homer (YFC)
- Ron Parker (Living Springs Camp)
- Taped message from Andrew Dunn.

Following the meal, Rev Cliff Dunn conducted a Thanksgiving Service with a theme of gratefulness for God's blessings, many of which cannot be measured in monetary terms.

The evening concluded with the AGM followed by updates of work supported by Waidale from Rev John McKinley of the Bible Society, Margaret Ischia and Geof Nicholson. Norman McIntosh of OMF then spoke, basing his message on Ecclesiastes 11:4-6: 'Whoever watches the wind will not plant; whoever looks at the clouds will not reap.'

# The Second Decade

1977–1987

## The Big Flood and Economic Factors

As the Trust entered its second decade there was every reason to look back and celebrate the faithfulness of God. In his 1977 Annual Report, Chairman Ron Paterson noted that over the previous period of ten years Waidale had given $160,000 to mission both in New Zealand and overseas. In the year 1976-1977 a figure of $24,314 had been distributed. It was as if they were entering a new phase of growth.

However, other events unfolded which affected many of the Waidale Trust members and supporters to varying degrees. These were years of uncertainty for farmers. Industrial disputes at freezing works caused mayhem in 1978. While the farmers waited, their sheep were starving and losing condition. In Invercargill, some farmers protested by taking their stock to town and marching with them through the CBD.

During the first half of 1978 there were only nine days on which all four of the Southland freezing works were operating. In total, there had been 116 recorded stoppages in the first five months of 1978, resulting in Southland's kill being about 700,000 behind that of the previous season, with one million head of stock still waiting to be killed and the season due to finish.[9]

In October 1978 a mammoth weather event affected the whole Mataura Valley and West Otago, causing what came to be known as the 100-year flood. Throughout the province everyone felt the impact whether they were farming or not.

Stock losses were heading towards 30,000 sheep, a similar number of lambs, 6,000 ewes and hoggets, 400 dairy cattle, 400 beef cattle and 900 beehives. Fence losses alone were about $2 million.[10]

**God's work done in God's way will never lack God's supply.**
– Hudson Taylor

Those not affected helped their neighbours who were. Yet, throughout these years of unpredictable returns and farming profits, the reputation of the Trust was spreading and support for the Trust did not diminish as names of new missionaries were being added to their growing list.

***

### Gordon and Roswitha Bayne

It was 1977 when Gordon Bayne was first introduced to Waidale by SIM director, Don Coop. After his application to the mission had been accepted, he was seeking support to go to Ethiopia. He can still remember the day he met Trust members at the home of Bruce and Ngaire Heslip. Because he had come from a sheep-farming

---

9. Fallow, M. (2013, May 7). *Southland Times*. Retrieved from http://www.stuff.co.nz/southland-times/news/8639392/Farmers-sheep-slaughter-protest-revisited

10. Lind, C. A. (1978). *The 100 year flood.* Invercargill, NZ: Craig Printing Co. Ltd.

background he felt at ease among these farmers from Southland as he shared his story, his call and his appointment, but the meeting was interrupted by a phone call with disturbing news. There had been a coup d'état in Ethiopia; a communist regime had taken power and expelled all missionaries from the country. Don Coop had to leave immediately to drive back to Auckland. But before he left, he asked Gordon if he had any thoughts about working in a different country. Gordon replied that he had always been interested in Benin. He knew Chris and Helen Cowie who were based there, although he was somewhat reluctant to work in a country where he would have to learn two languages. He was well aware that members of SIM often joked that the mission initials really meant *sure I'll move* and now it was as if that interpretation perfectly fitted his situation. What he did not know was that romance was also waiting in Benin and it was there he met Roswitha who was from Austria and had been working in literacy and language with the Betammaribe people. After their marriage in 1980 raising personal support was always a challenge so they were very grateful for regular Waidale contributions. It enabled them to buy their first vehicle – a Datsun double cabin ute – which was just what Gordon needed for his TEE (Theology Education by Extension) ministry with the Betammaribe churches. The work was multiplying very rapidly requiring Gordon to travel around an area approximately half the size of the South Island, often over very rough roads.

Once when some Waidale supporters visited them in Benin, they were a bit nervous travelling with Gordon when stock appeared on the road. He had learnt that driving in Africa meant understanding animal psychology: goats would run full speed across the road and never change their mind; sheep would just sit there, whereas guinea fowl were almost schizophrenic and likely to change their direction at the last minute.

Gordon and Roswitha believed the Waidale model was God-inspired and saw it replicated in Benin. One of the ethnic groups, the Fulani, had their own Bible College but was struggling to get their own people to support the ministry in spite of regularly pleading for funds. When Gordon explained how Waidale worked they were very open to trying the same model. The people were cattle herders and did not have a lot of cash on hand but they purchased some stock and asked Christian herdsmen to herd them with their own animals. Some years later Gordon learnt that the Bible School was now well financed. He realised it had given great confidence to the local believers who would have otherwise struggled to accomplish the task.

Gordon and Roswitha appreciated that, as well as providing finance, various Trust members kept in touch and remained up-to-date with their work.

***

### Bruce and Carol Symons

Bruce and Carol Symons have been supported by Waidale for many years. Bruce reflects:

> We have been members of Wycliffe Bible Translators[11] since 1978. We have worked in New Zealand, Solomon Islands, Papua New Guinea and Australia. Our main part in the overall task of Bible translation and literacy has been in training people in linguistics. We are always excited to see people learning skills they need to help communities translate and use the Bible. It

---

11. Wycliffe Bible Translators New Zealand has the purpose 'to see the Scriptures made available through Bible translation to all peoples in the language they know best.' http://wycliffenz.org/about/who-we-are/purpose/

### Farming with a smile

One story has always stayed with Gordon:

Being farmers, the Waidale men were always looking at practical ways they could help us. Once we had a problem keeping livestock away from the fields forcing many to have their fields long distances away. When Waidale heard of the problem, Richard White offered to buy us an electric fence unit. Because it was a problem keeping the fence clear of elephant grass the batteries charging the fence weren't used quite in the way I had planned. However, it proved useful in an unexpected situation. One night Roswitha and I were stung by a scorpion. Our guard prayed for us but it was still painful. Local people believed that touching the sting site with an electric shock was helpful. Well, we realised we couldn't touch something on the mains current but (ha ha), we had an electric fence unit going; that should do the trick. So there we were in our pyjamas, standing in front of the wire, exhorting each other to touch it. Ouch! Maybe that wasn't quite enough. Once more! Oww!! There wasn't any immediate radical change but it was most unusual that we could to go back to bed and soon fall asleep. Often people suffered for up to 24 hours whereas our recovery was much faster.

has been a special privilege when we hear about Scripture being used in different parts of the world – from Mexico to India, Papua New Guinea to Mozambique, New Caledonia to countries in the Middle East.

Since the early days of our time with Wycliffe, the trustees of Waidale Trust have generously and faithfully supported us. Thus they have shared significantly in this task. For us as a family their support often came at crucial times: school fees, dentist bills, car repairs, and visits to New Zealand. We thank God for his faithfulness to us through the Trust.

***

### Celebrations and a Growing Number of Missions

In addition to regular meetings and business, celebrations were a popular addition to the Trust calendar. In 1980 the first Waidale Christmas party was held at the home of Jim and Janice McNamara. It was an excellent evening with members, supporters, spouses and families numbering approximately seventy adults plus children. A shared meal was followed by carol singing, updates from missionaries, a Christmas devotional message from Gordon Homer and a brief insight into the Lay Institute for Evangelism by Janice's father, Doug Malcolm. The Christmas parties continued for some years, but more recently the AGM has proved to be an appropriate opportunity to celebrate with supporters. An evening with a meal and listening to missionary speakers has become a highlight.

In 1982 the Trust sponsored a visit from well-known Bible teacher Rev Graham Miller. He was the speaker at the Bible Class Easter camp at Camp Columba, Pukerau.

Missions and missionaries supported during these years included:

- The Bible College of New Zealand was grateful for funds enabling them to appoint staff for their newly developed Missions Department.
- Christian Youth Camps Inc. – known as CYC – appreciated funding for Christian camps held at their site at Waihola near Dunedin.
- Navigators were grateful for funding as they pursued their national and international mission focus of evangelism and discipleship for tertiary students as well as helping churches to prepare and mobilise Christians for mission throughout the world.
- OMF International – A mission with a pioneer focus on reaching the people of East Asia was founded as the China Inland Mission by Hudson Taylor in 1865. Margaret Wyber was one of those supported.
- Pounawea Convention – It was at the Keswick convention at Pounawea where the idea for Waidale was conceived.
- Scripture Union – works with churches to create opportunities for children and young people to discover and follow Jesus, grow as leaders and influence our world.
- Tertiary Students Christian Fellowship (TSCF), formerly Intervarsity Fellowship, encourages students through intentional discipleship to grow as leaders and apply their faith to all areas of their life.
- Worldwide Evangelisation Crusade (WEC) – now Worldwide Evangelisation for Christ – was founded in 1913 by CT Studd, and the mission adopted his motto: 'If Jesus Christ be God and died for me, then no sacrifice can be too great for me to make for him.'

- Youth for Christ (YFC) pioneered Campus Life Clubs in high schools, Rock Solid groups in intermediate schools and Te Hou Ora clubs for 'at risk' young people.
- Camp Columba at Pukerau was established in 1954 and was supported by Harry White's Otama Trust in 1958 when it was facing financial crisis. Harry shared his vision with Waidale members, many of whom were already involved helping to erect the buildings at the camp site. The spiritual impact of camps held there, both in mission and evangelism, has been immeasurable and Waidale support for Camp Columba continues today.

***

### Balancing Change and Continuity: Jim Weir and Ron Paterson

As the years progressed, there were some further changes of roles and responsibilities within the Trust. When Jim McNamara stepped down as secretary in 1981, Jim Weir was elected to the position. He had been inspired by mission all of his life. He grew up hearing stories of his paternal grandparents who had worked as Presbyterian missionaries in the New Hebrides (now Vanuatu). His understanding of mission was further inspired by the example of Clarence Gardyne and Harry White and their unreserved commitment to the Waidale Trust. His father grazed stock to support Waidale. Jim noticed how their own local church vision was enlarged because of the missionaries who visited. He also noticed the positive impact on the lives of the youth in the parish through groups like Youth for Christ.

Since his election as a trustee in 1978 his interest in missions has expanded and he has been greatly encouraged that Waidale has a focus on people rather than the organisation they represent. During the seven years he was secretary he spent quite a lot of time with Harry White. Over the course of an afternoon or an evening together they would write cheques which were sent to various recipients along with a letter. As the list of the people supported by the Trust grew, the volume of mail received meant an equally larger volume of replies were needed. So when Jim was asked to consider taking on the position of parish treasurer, he knew he couldn't do both roles. When he resigned, Elinor Collins was elected but Jim has remained as a trustee. He continues to graze stock to support Waidale on his his mixed beef, sheep and cropping farm at East Chatton.

Twenty years after Waidale was established, the 1987 worldwide share market crash hit farmers and landowners everywhere. It could have derailed support, but it did not. Through all of these changes, one man chaired the Trust.

Ron Paterson was elected chairman at the beginning of the Trust, and continued in the chair for thirty years. He grew up on a farm near Waikaka and had known many of the Waidale Trust members since he was young. As teenagers, Clarence Gardyne and Ron were part of 'the gang', a group who got on so well together they would arrange their own trips away to places such as Queenstown or Stewart Island. At different times, many of them also served on the District Committee which organised Easter camps. Their friendships lasted into their adult lives, and extended into their years on the Waidale Trust.

After his marriage to Dulcie, Ron farmed sheep, beef and deer on 6000 acres (2428 ha) at Moonlight Station, nestled at the foot of East Dome in the Garvie Mountains. Although he had attended many Pounawea Conventions, he wasn't there when the Dunns shared their story.

**God's choice acquaintances are humble men.**
– Robert Leighton

But he soon heard about them at the next Riversdale session meeting when Harry tabled the idea of stock fundraising as a means of support for the family. Ron knew Harry was a man of action so it was no surprise when it was decided to establish a committee to oversee the project, with representatives from both Riversdale and Waikaka parishes. Ron and Harry were both elected onto the committee. Ron had a quieter nature than Harry, but they shared similar values, especially in regard to mission. A few months later, when the Waidale Trust was established, Ron was elected chairman. He doesn't remember exactly how it happened but he was willing and held the position for thirty years. He recalls that in those early days not everyone was keen on the idea of trading in stock and some preferred to give a donation. But most soon realised that grazing stock was a more effective way of raising the required funding. Their efforts to support mission proved to be especially significant because of the disquiet within the wider church caused by the Geering controversy.[12] But the Trust members were adamant that the outcome of that matter would not derail their efforts to support mission. They were also very conscious that, although the funds came from raising sheep and cattle, the people who grazed them needed to know just where their money was going.

Waidale was a considerable time commitment. It would have taken about half an hour for Ron to drive to each meeting, held either at Wendon or Otama. Over the years, as the number of applications for funding increased, the meetings were rarely finished before midnight. In those days everything was written by

12. In 1967 Professor Lloyd Geering, Principal of Knox College, publicly denied the bodily resurrection of Jesus Christ and questioned the supernatural attributes of God. He was charged with heresy and doctrinal error at the General Assembly of the Presbyterian Church of New Zealand. Many church members resigned, resulting in a significant decline in finance and support for both the local church and mission.

hand, correspondence and letters were read out in full at each meeting and prayerful discussion took a long time. His wife Dulcie was not fazed: 'Farmers are farmers and they love to talk after the meetings.' She remembers lying in bed, dozing off to sleep but waking often until she knew Ron had arrived home and his head was on the pillow beside her.

In his 1987 annual report, Ron was able to record that the Trust donations during the previous year had totalled $90,004.

### Farming with a smile

Support for Waidale sometimes came from an unexpected source. On one occasion Ron's neighbour, from Glenlapa station, phoned to say some of Ron's stock had wandered onto his property. When Ron realised it was Waidale stock it opened up an unexpected opportunity to tell his neighbour about the Trust. Andrew Dunn just happened to be visiting Ron and Dulcie at the time, so it seemed like a natural progression to invite the neighbour to meet him. Andrew clearly remembers sitting around the table at the Patersons' as he chatted about the work he and Margaret were doing in Papua New Guinea. The neighbour was so inspired by the story he offered to run some stock to support Waidale.

*Top: Clarence and Margaret Gardyne.*
*Bottom: Margery and Harry White.*

*Top: Andrew and Margaret Dunn with Stephen, Lynne, Cathy and Karen. Easter 1977 at Varirata National Park near Port Moresby. Bottom: Andrew and Margaret Dunn.*

*Top: A presentation to Dulcie and Ron Paterson on the occasion of Ron's retirement from the Trust in 2010. Bottom: George Simpson accepting a minute of appreciation from the Trust on his retirement in 2014.*

*Top: George and Diane Cook.*
*Bottom: Gordon and Elinor Collins.*

*Waidale Trustees 1994. Standing from left: Gordon Collins, David Smith, Bruce Roy, Jim Weir, Graeme Gardyne, Richard White, John Wilson, Betty Smith, John Gardyne, Bruce Heslip, John Kerse. Sitting: Don Tayles, Stan Clark, Clarence Gardyne, George Simpson. At table: Ron Paterson (Chairman) Elinor Collins (Secretary). Absent: Cliff Clark, John Moore, Keith Halliday, Dirkje Kelly, Hamish Mackay, Basil Paterson, Neil Jackson, Margery White.*

*Waidale Trustees 2007. Back Row: John Kerse, Graeme Gardyne, John Gardyne. Middle Row: John Wilson, David Smith, Richard White, Jim Weir, Doug Dodds, Hamish Mackay, Bruce Heslip. Front Row: Keith Halliday, Elinor Collins (Secretary), Gordon Collins, Betty Smith, George Cook (Chairman), Ron Paterson, Margery White, Clarence Gardyne, George Simpson.*

*Top: Amy and Norman McIntosh.*
*Bottom left: Alan and Averil Bennett. Bottom right: Kristina and John Tipper with Micah, Larissa, Adelle.*

*Top: George Simpson and Willie Heenan tailing at Gracevale.*
*Bottom: 14-month Angus cross steer calves at Gracevale.*

# The Third Decade

1987–1997

## Passing On the Baton: from Harry White to Richard White and Graeme Gardyne

As the third decade began, Harry White continued in his role as stock manager and treasurer, with enthusiasm and commitment. But sadly, due to declining health, he was unable to continue. His immense contribution of more than twenty-two years was appropriately honoured with a Life Membership at the AGM in July 1989.

He knew the time had come to pass on the baton. Expecting someone else to take full responsibility for both stock and finances was a tall order. The solution was to split the role into two parts. He asked his son Richard to take on the financial management because he had a good head for figures. Richard began to attend Waidale meetings and gradually understood how the established processes worked. It is a role he still enjoys doing today, but it is not all paperwork: he grazes cattle for the Trust on his 1800-acre (728.4 ha) sheep and beef farm at Wendonside and continues to have a vested interest in the home block at Otama.

Graeme Gardyne accepted the responsibility for stock management. Over a period of time he learnt the art from Harry as they went together to sales all around Southland. The trips were never boring because as they travelled Harry would talk with great enthusiasm about stock and about Waidale opportunities. One trip was memorable for the wrong reasons: Graeme has never forgotten that day when they were heading home after a sale at Castle Rock. He was so engrossed with what Harry was saying as they drove into Lumsden, he forgot to reduce his speed and was ticketed by a traffic officer.

Whenever Harry knew people who were selling or buying stock or property he would look for an opportunity for Waidale to have some involvement. Graeme remembers that both Harry and Clarence were known to have suggested to other Waidale graziers 'If you had that other block of land you could run some more stock for Waidale.'

Graeme and his brother John are thankful that their father encouraged them to be part of Waidale and that it has been part of their lives from a young age. Clarence was a positive role model, not only for his sons, but for others too. Richard and Rob White remember him as a prayerful man, who was wise, strong, faithful and godly, and who was always interested in what they were doing.

Waidale's stock management has changed over the years. An increase in dairying in Southland has changed the face of farming there. Twenty years ago there were a lot more beef calves but now their number has decreased. The need to attend sales regularly has diminished but when Graeme does purchase stock he knows it is important to match the right class of stock to the right property. Now the graziers make a lot of the decisions and so the scheme tends to be self-managing. Farmers are happy to buy their own stock and set aside some for Waidale. Many graziers have standing arrangements and consistently purchase from the same person. The balance between stock numbers and profit margin has shifted too. Harry would handle larger numbers of cattle on a smaller margin, whereas now there are fewer cattle but a bigger margin.

When Waidale began, few such schemes existed. But now schools, churches and sports clubs have discovered this is an effective way to raise funds. It means that sometimes it takes more work to raise support. It is important to keep the vision alive for the next generation but that brings its own challenges because of the large capital investment younger farmers need to make to buy a property. A few years ago a grazing block could be purchased for a reasonable price but as more dairy farmers look for run-off blocks, prices have become much more competitive.

Graeme is always conscious that Waidale needs to be a positive experience for the people involved and it is important to work with them to achieve a good outcome. Sometimes there are unexpected challenges, such as putting heifers out for grazing then discovering they are in calf. The recent outbreak of Mycoplasma bovis on some farms in other parts of Southland has heightened awareness among Trust members of the need to be vigilant and careful with stock movement. Yet despite the difficulties, the vision continues. Graeme reflects:

> It never ceases to amaze me how it all comes together. There has been a great spirit among the people involved in Waidale and some real commitment. People are very generous. They could do it as individuals but the fact they are doing it together is mutually encouraging. It is something we need to make sure we preserve.

Harry White certainly left a legacy when he passed away in January 1990 and a fitting tribute of appreciation was recorded in the minutes:

> [Harry's] unique business and stock-handling talents made a very significant contribution in ensuring that the Trust became

> God's instrument in meeting the financial needs of many who are engaged in proclaiming the Gospel of Christ. It was a responsibility that he undertook with humility, perseverance and dedication. Harry's advice and guidance at Trust meetings, as discussions centred on many requests that were presented, indicated that he was the one who was willing to look at fresh opportunities in presenting the Gospel.

The growth of the Trust continued to be exceptional. As they prepared to celebrate the twenty-fifth anniversary in 1992, there were twenty-seven trustees and fifty supporters spread throughout West Otago, and Eastern and Northern Southland. Funds available for distribution in the 1991-1992 year had reached $131,670 and, although the profits from sheep were falling, the profits from cattle were rising. One hundred and ten people gathered in Riversdale for the thanksgiving service and celebration dinner.

***

### George Simpson and Gracevale

At the time of the silver anniversary, another exciting development was being considered: the purchase of land and buildings. During the twenty-five years the Waidale Trust had been in existence they had never owned property, nor did they aspire to do so. However, that was all to change in a most unexpected way.

In the heart of the Wendon Valley you will find Old Church Corner, where Clinker Valley Road and the Waikaka-Wendon roads meet. In years gone by the T-intersection was a meeting place, a busy hub of activity for families. The location is marked by two storyboards which recount how children were educated for sixty years in the 27 by 21 foot schoolroom. On Sundays it was trans-

**Twenty-fifth Anniversary**

14 November 1992

Theme: The blessings of God

Venue: Thanksgiving service – Riversdale Presbyterian Church. Dinner – Riversdale Community Centre

Special guests:

- Rev Cliff Dunn and Norman McIntosh
- Rev Andrew and Margaret Dunn (first missionaries supported by the Trust)
- Murray Dunn (NZ Director SIM International)

Some of the guests who had been at both the inaugural meeting of the Trust and the tenth anniversary were present at the Silver Jubilee celebrations.

- At the church service Rev Andrew Dunn preached about the need to follow Jesus closely. As we draw near to Christ we must let go of everything else and come with open and repentant hearts. The service concluded with communion.
- At the dinner Norman McIntosh spoke of the value of missionaries having their hands strengthened by others, just as David's hands were strengthened by Jonathan (1 Samuel 23:16).
- Rev Cliff Dunn shared how his parish ministry

and vision among his people had been positively impacted by mission. For he and his wife it had begun by hearing the stories from missionaries they had hosted in their home.

- Mrs Margery White cut the cake, and spoke of the blessing that had come to their family through hosting missionaries in their home.
- Murray Dunn challenged the young men and women to take up the responsibilities of the Trust and to commit to continue the vision of the Trust founders.

Graeme Gardyne, one of the younger members of the Trust, proposed a vote of thanks.

Prayer and singing the doxology concluded the evening.

formed into a church. But after forty-four years of worshipping there and in other venues, parishioners in 1929 opened a brand new 'small but handsome' wooden church on the opposite side of the road. Worship in the new building continued for a further thirty-four years, yet the final service in November 1963 did not mark the end of its useful life. Since 1965 it has served as a chapel at Camp Columba at Pukerau, a ministry regularly supported by the Waidale Trust.

The first settlers in the valley between Waikaka and Chatton discovered it held treasures of its own. A concise description has been recorded on the storyboards for future generations: 'Watered by its many springs and the Waikaka Stream this area is known for its fertile soil, snowgrass tussocks and gold.'

**George Simpson**, the first secretary of the Trust, knew a good farm when he saw one. Six years before Waidale Trust was established he found just such a property in the Wendon Valley, and decided to purchase the 319-acre (129 ha) block, located quite close to Old Church Corner. George had grown up on a farm near Waikaka with his twin brother Jim, and younger brother Raymond. Their family attended the Waikaka Presbyterian church. He loved farming and enjoyed the challenge of playing rugby (referred to in those days as football). He discovered that Bible Class, church and district social activities, as well as camps, were great places to make friends – but doing anything that might take him too far out of his comfort zone did not appeal. He always imagined he would marry and settle down with a family but life is not always predictable. One day his thoughts and dreams were interrupted. He was a young man in a Bible Class being led by Rev G. McKenzie. That evening he was teaching about the importance of being willing to be fully obedient to God's call on our lives. The idea of commencing studies to train for the ministry popped into George's head. 'Where did that come from?' he wondered. 'Was it God's voice nudging me or was it simply a random thought?' It was not a direction aligned to his natural inclination and he felt inadequate for such a task. The thought did not go away. For six months he wrestled with the implications of such a move. It was indeed a clash of wills: he kept reminding God how much he loved farming. God kept reminding him of the words in 1 Corinthians 6:19-20, 'You are not your own, you have been bought at a price.' George didn't want to become a public figure in any sense of the word. God kept reassuring him from Hebrews 13:5 (NKJV), 'I will never leave you nor forsake you.' After six months of praying, seeking counsel from Rev McKenzie, and pursuing the idea he decided that although he felt very nervous about the prospect, he was willing to say yes to God. And then a strange thing happened: the desire left him; it fell away like an old coat. It was a significant experience in his personal journey of faith and a worthwhile lesson which has endured as a hallmark throughout his life. And God certainly was not silent in the years to come.

One evening, just a few days after he had taken possession of his new property, he was walking back to the sheds when he had the strong impression that in the future his farm would become a trust. Such an idea seemed incomprehensible to George, but rather than dismissing it completely, he simply kept it in his heart and pondered it. Once more he wondered if it was God's voice or simply a random thought. Little did he know what sequence of events would unfold in the future.

**He is no fool who gives what he cannot keep, to gain what he cannot lose.**
– Jim Elliot

Thirty years later, as retirement beckoned, it would have been logical for him to sell the farm and invest the money, but instead he remembered the thought that had come to him that evening all those years before. George tentatively asked one or two Trust members if they thought Waidale would consider leasing his farm. It generated some very worthwhile and positive discussion before he decided to submit the proposition formally to the Trust. After further consideration, a small committee formalised the agreement for a lease, with the provision that a full and thorough review be conducted prior to the end of the lease period. It was unanimously agreed to accept the offer and on 1 September 1991 the first three-year term began.

John Gardyne accepted responsibility for overseeing the property on behalf of the Trust. In subsequent years he and his wife Jo, as well as David Smith have invested a lot of time working with the manager and lessees to bring improvements to the farm.

As the end of the first lease period approached, it was obvious that taking on Gracevale had been a wise decision. As agreed, the finances had remained quite separate from the Trust, and the balance sheet proved it was economically viable. Employing a manager had created a very workable partnership. George decided that the time was now right to offer the farm for sale to the Trust. It was a significant move which was the culmination of a lifetime of obedience. When George first sensed God was calling him to full-time ministry, he had no idea that his investment in a farm would support the ministry of others. The parallel is profound: for thirty years George farmed his property before offering it to the Trust to be used in mission. It has impacted successive generations. Likewise, Jesus spent thirty years preparing for ministry, which has impacted every generation throughout time. The name *Gracevale*, which George had chosen, is such an appropriate name.

**Stuart and Shona Davie.** The same year that George first offered his farm for lease, Stuart and Shona Davie were working on a stud Angus cattle farm near Geraldine in South Canterbury. They'd both grown up on Southland farms, Shona at Waimumu and Stuart at Waikoikoi. Their two families knew each other well. So when Stuart was offered a bank transfer from Invercargill to Timaru at about the same time as Shona's parents returned to a family farm in the Timaru district, their friendship of many years led to marriage. In spite of good prospects in the corporate world, Stuart felt restless and began to wish he was back on the land. The perfect opportunity came when they successfully applied for the position at Geraldine. Less than a year later the idea of returning to Southland was mentioned casually in conversation with their friends the Mackays. The idea began to resonate more strongly a few months later when Waidale trustee, Bruce Heslip, phoned them with a proposal. He explained that the Trust had acquired the lease of a farm at Wendon

Valley and asked if they would be interested in managing the property. They knew about Waidale because Hamish Mackay's father, Lewis, was a foundation trustee. But for Stuart and Shona there were many factors to consider. It would mean a major shift: their young son, Justin, was eighteen months old and they were expecting their second baby. The move would take them back closer to Stuart's family but they would be leaving Shona's family behind. This unexpected change of direction required careful and prayerful consideration. They decided it was worth pursuing and headed south to check it out. Stuart felt an immediate connection with Bruce Heslip, and Clarence, John and Graeme Gardyne, who met with them. These men had an enthusiasm and passion for Waidale, which was almost infectious, as they talked of mission and showed them around the Wendon Valley property.

Stuart and Shona's first impression was of a beautiful little farm and an exciting opportunity for them to work together. Shona loved farming too, so it was an ideal situation. Everything seemed right so they decided to accept the offer. There was a six-week gap between resigning from their job in Geraldine and moving south. So when Shona's father injured his knee just before lambing they were free to help him. They believed that God works in every circumstance for good and for them it seemed perfect timing. But during those six weeks their faith was to be put to a much more difficult test. Nothing could have prepared them for the moment which seems forever frozen in time. Stuart recalls it as if it had happened yesterday: 'It was a Saturday night when we got the phone call to say Fraser had been killed.'

Fraser was Stuart's younger brother and had been killed in a car accident. The lives of the whole Davie family were thrown into the turbulence of incomprehensible grief. Stuart and Shona were touched deeply by support from the trustees, many of whom attended Fraser's funeral.

Because Stuart's older brother had just married and moved to Wellington, Stuart and Shona were now absolutely sure that their decision was the right one. Their move meant they would be the only immediate family members living close to his parents.

Resolutely they continued with their plans for moving to Wendon Valley. Stuart arrived first and Shona followed shortly afterwards. In the following months they drew strength and hope from God, enabling them to somehow make it through the aftermath of the tragedy. The pain of loss was mixed with the joy of reconnecting with school friends and families they had known while growing up. It was a little bit like coming home.

### Farming with a smile

On the first day of work it was tailing time on the farm, a day which Stuart hasn't forgotten:

> The day I arrived, George Simpson came with Stan Clark and Ron Paterson to start into tailing. The first day went fine. The next day, first thing in the morning, Ron Paterson was rolling out the netting backwards down the fence line, and he didn't see the trough behind him. It caught his leg at the back and he sat down with a splash. Everyone thought it was very funny, except Ron. It was right at the start of the day so he had to work for the rest of the day in soaking wet trousers. It looked really funny. I will never forget that.

As they settled in, they appreciated improvements made by the Trust. In the house, the existing fire was replaced with a Yunca multi-fuel unit, which was excellent during colder weather, especially with a baby and a toddler. John Gardyne worked with Stuart and Shona to plan and implement drainage work on the farm which improved the pasture quality and proved to be a great asset, especially during the winter months.

The farm was recognised among the neighbours as an excellent fattening property. Many of them were surprised when they learnt of George's decision to offer it to Waidale. For the Davies, it made them very conscious that there was a reputation to uphold as a good neighbour and that community involvement was important. Helping to lead the local youth group suited them and the farm was an ideal venue for some of their activities. During those years the Waikaka Presbyterian church held an annual pony trek and the farm was a regular stopping place.

Because the property was good for fattening stock, buying in store lambs from higher altitude locations such as Glenary Station, bringing them down country to the rich pasture in the valley proved to be a profitable exercise. One year when cattle prices were down Stuart took some rising two-year-old heifers into the Charlton sale. He had wintered them over, and he knew they were in good condition but he was also aware there was a general downturn in stock prices. Bidding at the sale was brisk, stretched between the few buyers present. Many of the purchasers were local butchers and Stuart was quite astonished when the heifers fetched top price of the day at $750 each. Occasions like this reminded him that although he was responsible for managing the farm, it was always God who guided his steps.

Like all farmers, they still encountered problems. One spring was memorable for all the wrong reasons. Stuart remembers it well.

> One lambing we got hammered with bearing trouble. I will never forget it. It got to the stage you didn't want to go out the door because there would be all these bearings to deal with. Probably the ewes were in too good a nick coming out of the winter. It was just a bad year for it, and it meant a low lambing percentage, but not just for us. We also had some sheep stolen at one stage. Between pre-lamb crutching and lambing time we lost about 150 ewes. That was quite a lot for a wee place. Some other sheep around the district went missing about the same time.

Farming provides an opportunity to share equipment and tasks with neighbours. Stuart and Shona worked in with Steve and Judi Dennis next door to do tailing and share implements. Steve would borrow Stuart's ridger. Stuart sometimes needed a bigger tractor. Their children were of similar ages so they had much in common and their friendship has continued throughout the years.

Because it was a small block, the Trustees gave Stuart the freedom to do other work. He established himself as an agricultural contractor and as the dairy conversion boom took off, there was always plenty of work.

Stuart and Shona continued to manage Gracevale until 1996. They loved the venture but after five years they felt their season had come to an end. Their departure closed a door in their lives but opened an opportunity for another person who was available at just the right time.

**Willie and Mairi Heenan.** Willie Heenan first came to New Zealand in 1979, as a student on placement from the United Kingdom, and was based in West Otago. He first heard about Waidale through his involvement in Bible Class at Tapanui and Crookston, led by Mervyn Muir and Murray McKenzie. Little did he know the part it would play in his life in future years. When his placement ended, he went back to the United Kingdom but returned again to Crookston in 1993 to manage a farm there. Three years later, when he was on the verge of leaving for a short trip to visit his parents in Northern Ireland, he received a phone call asking if he would consider managing the Wendon Valley property. Willie sensed that God was opening a door and he felt excited at this unexpected opportunity to support mission in New Zealand and overseas. His interest in mission had grown over many years and now he could contribute in a very fulfilling way. He began managing Gracevale in October 1996 and, like the Davies, the first job was tailing. He takes up the story:

> Working together gave me the opportunity to get to know my neighbours. The fellowship and friendship of George Simpson, with his knowledge of the farm and his willingness to help, was a great asset in helping me settle into life in Wendon Valley. I appreciated the help too from visits to John and Jo Gardyne's home for the regular GST returns, not to mention the home cooking that went along with it.'

Willie became involved with the wider community. Through his role as an Officer with the Waikoikoi Boys' Brigade he came to know a lot of the boys from the Waikaka church. They would often work for him during holidays doing tasks like tailing, drenching, crutching lambs and topping paddocks, which is mowing thistles and grass which has gone to seed. Waidale Trust then offered Willie the opportunity to lease the farm. For Willie, it was God's timely provision to enable him to develop his farming career; it gave him the opportunity to build up his own stock numbers, diversify into rearing calves and run a contracting business. There were some other changes in Willie's life:

> Unknown to the Trust, there was another attraction back in Scotland! Mairi and I had met back in Aberdeen in 1990 and when I emigrated to New Zealand we had kept in touch by snail mail and long landline phone calls—it was before the days of texting or skype! We were married in Aberdeen in 2000 and returned to New Zealand from our honeymoon straight into lambing and calf rearing! We hosted a steady stream of family members and friends at Gracevale Farm over the next number of years.

As well as farming, Mairi was teaching at Waikaka School and Willie continued to be involved with Boys' Brigade, both locally and nationally. They were both involved in the Tapanui church and Mairi led the Banana Club, an after-school Bible club held alternatively at Knapdale and Otama.

Their time at Gracevale was a season of opportunities both on the farm and in the community. They loved living in the Wendon Valley and knew they were blessed, but then God stopped them in their tracks. His challenge for them was to move into full-time Christian ministry. As they prayed about it, the sense of God's call became stronger and they knew obedience was the only response. They began to work out the practicalities of what the move would mean. Their lease expired at the end of 2003 and they decided not to renew it. Instead they began planning for a clearing sale the following March. Willie finishes the story:

> The strange part of it all was that the previous season we had put the rams out earlier than usual, resulting in having the best lambing ever the following Spring, followed by an exceptional growing season. This, in God's provision, miraculously enabled us to have all our lambs fattened in our last season and off to the works by the middle of March. The clearing sale should

have been an emotional day but we found that we were carried through it and had a great inner peace and sense of God's hand in it all. Returning to the United Kingdom involved theological studies and church placements and I was then ordained and inducted to Parish Ministry. I have served in churches in Glasgow and now in Stornoway in the Hebrides.

We are so thankful for our time in Wendon Valley and look back with very fond memories of our time on Gracevale Farm. It will always hold a special place in our hearts as a place of peace with a real sense of God's presence. It is a unique ministry supporting mission work around the world and we are thankful that in His providence, God enabled us to have a small part in this.

**Steve and Judi Dennis.** Current lessees Steve and Judi Dennis treat Gracevale as an extension of their own 900-acre (364 ha) farm on Clinker Hill Road. Just one property separates Gracevale from their property, Coalbrook, but they did not know anything about the Waidale Trust before they moved to the valley in May 1992.

Steve and Judi grew up, met and married in the Waimakariri District in North Canterbury. They were keen to keep farming but wanted to exchange the small blocks they owned for a larger property. Steve used to joke that they could move south, but Judi never took him seriously. She kept trying to persuade him to look in other areas closer to home. In retrospect, they have no doubt that God led them to the district, even though it meant leaving family behind in Darfield and Oxford. Steve first felt attracted to the south when he had driven down with a mate who was looking for work. After strong nor'westers and droughts in Canterbury he couldn't help but notice the good condition of the stock in Southland, and the rolling lie of the land appealed to him. Fifteen years after his first visit, Steve and Judi signed up to purchase Coalbrook. They had barely finished unpacking when Stuart and Shona Davie came to make themselves known. Judi recalls the moment:

> There was a knock on the door and this young couple was standing there. They had two little boys: Justin was two years and Simon was three months. I asked to hold the baby. We really clicked with them. It was an immediate friendship.

That friendship helped them to settle into the area. From the beginning, there were many occasions when the two families could share the workload. Their children were similar ages so tailing was very much a family affair. For other farm tasks such as sowing, ploughing, fencing, and drilling, they found that sharing equipment was an ideal arrangement. They would help each other out if there was a problem. One day, while trying to put fence posts in, Stuart got bogged near the creek so Steve went down with the bulldozer to rescue him. And if one family went away on holiday, the other was happy to look after their farm.

As Steve and Judi settled they liked what they saw of Gracevale. Being involved with mission was very familiar to both of them. Steve's parents had spent time in the Solomon Islands in mission work where his dad had helped to set up sawmills. Judi had spent time overseas on two short-term mission stints. So the idea of being part of the Waidale vision appealed. After Stuart and Shona left, they built up a good relationship with Willie Heenan. He would often come for tea on Friday night which was Brigade night at Waikoikoi. The girls met in the church hall, the boys met in the community hall and Willie was happy to drive Steve and Judi's daughter Rebecca there each week. When their boys, Andy and Jon were older, they would go down and help Willie with calf rearing. He was a great mentor for the boys.

When Willie and Mairi Heenan decided to return to the United

Kingdom, Steve and Judi were sorry to see them go, but were delighted that it gave them an opportunity to tender for the lease. Judi felt as if God had told them they would be farming Gracevale so they were disappointed to learn their offer was unsuccessful. For the next eighteen months, brothers Rob and John Hall of Halland Downs leased the farm but, due to unforeseen circumstances, they were unable to complete their three-year term. So Steve and Judi were asked if they would be interested in a sub-lease since their original tender had been the second in line. They jumped at the opportunity and since 2010 have leased the property.

They have found that working Gracevale is very much a partnership with the Waidale Trust. They feel supported and have an open relationship with Trust members. They have appreciated practical advice from George Simpson and learnt from his wisdom. They are actively involved in the Knapdale-Waikaka Presbyterian parish, which provides an ideal platform to connect with some of the other Trust members, especially John Gardyne, Jim Weir and David Smith. During their tenure they have developed the property, especially fencing and drainage. They have cleared out a lot of old crack willow, which had got out of control along the rivers, and dealt with rogue broom, gorse and barley grass. They have continued the care and protection of the tussock and wetland area which gives shelter during lambing and helps to keep the waterways clean.

From the commencement of the lease they have farmed the two properties as one unit, because Gracevale and Coalbrook complement each other. Gracevale is excellent as a fattening property and finishing block. The ewes there lamb first, fatten quickly and can be sold off quite early in the season. When the Gracevale lambs have gone, Steve and Judi can move the Coalbrook-born lambs down there. Running the two blocks as one allows them to share grazing and has enabled them to engage in pastoral renewal. Currently both properties are farmed for beef, sheep, cereal and winter feed crops.

All the shearing is now done at Coalbrook and Judi prepares the meals. They use local labour in the sheds when they can. In the winter of 2017, Gracevale was running 1,104 terminal ewes, 65 young beef cattle and 700 two-tooth ewes on winter feed. They were cropping an area of 8 hectares.

Both Steve and Judi have a passion for farming and share the work equally. Judi loves to encourage women in farming but she also loves being involved in ministry. Many individuals have come to stay on the farm for time out and healing which has been a fulfilment of the prayers of one of the previous owners of Coalbrook, Jim and Allison Wescombe. Before leaving the farm they had prayed that it would continue to be a place of ministry and a place of reconciliation.

Although Judi took a while to settle in the south, she has recently discovered stronger family links to Southland than she realised: her great, great uncle Moses McLay farmed at the top of the Wendon Valley while his brother – her great, great grandfather, also named Moses McLay – was once the postmaster at Merino Downs and an elder in their local church. Both Steve and Judi consider it a privilege to farm Gracevale and appreciate being stewards of such a beautiful farm.

***

### Elinor Collins: Trust member 1988–, Secretary 1988–2008

Unlike most of the trustees, Elinor neither grew up in Southland, nor in a Christian home, but she did understand farming. She grew up on a dairy farm close to Auckland, at Pukekohe East, where she also went to Sunday school with a friend, but only when she was old enough to bike there on her own. Although her parents did not have a Christian faith, it did not stop Elinor discovering her own personal relationship with God.

Her first visit to the south was by means of a Mitsubishi Silver Pigeon four-stroke automatic motor scooter, which she rode all the way to Invercargill. This intrepid traveller was not disheartened by a few road adventures with much bigger vehicles en route, but she was still pleased to meet her girlfriend in Christchurch. She was ready for adventure, but not prepared for the icicles hanging from the rocks around Alexandra. Four years later, after handing in her notice from her job at a local pharmacy, she headed back to Dunedin, this time to the Presbyterian Deaconess College. Life took some unexpected turns and, after recuperating from illness, Elinor took up a job housekeeping. She had no idea that fifteen years later it would lead to marriage and serving as secretary of The Waidale Trust. Her first introduction occurred when she went to work for the White family at the Otama homestead. During her eight years there she was responsible for serving supper at the conclusion of the Waidale meetings, which often went late into the night. She remembers that Harry had no qualms about pausing meeting proceedings to answer the telephone, which was located in a cupboard between the kitchen and living room.

Elinor and Gordon Collins first met at a missionary meeting at Otama. Romance soon blossomed and they were married in 1980. Eight years later she was approached and asked to take on the role of secretary of the Trust. After prayerful consideration she believed the timing was right and she agreed. She remembers the evening when Jim and Glenys Weir visited, bringing with them several boxes containing relevant records and minutes. As he put them down Jim declared 'This is Waidale.' Elinor had previously been a secretary for the Mataura Presbyterial[13] so she adapted to

---

13. A *presbyterial* is an elected committee of women within an area, each member representing her local church group or Association of Presbyterian Women.

the role quite quickly, though has never forgotten an embarrassing error when she once wrote a cheque incorrectly. She inadvertently added an extra zero to the amount. When the error became obvious, she imagined she might be dismissed, but instead the Trustees responded most graciously. After Gordon was elected as a trustee he proved to be a great support but she always asked him to verify each cheque and to proofread each letter before she posted them.

Elinor comments on her time as secretary:

> We held the meetings in our home and we modernised a few things. Up until this time the minutes had been handwritten. I began typing them on an electric typewriter, then later upgraded to a computer. Correspondence was also upgraded from all letters being put in a cardboard box in the middle of the room where everyone helped themselves, to producing a *guff sheet* where letters received were all photocopied and a copy was printed for each trustee to take home and digest.

***

## Support from Spouses

Throughout the fifty years of its existence, four couples have served together on the Waidale Trust: Harry and Margery White, Hamish and Miriam Mackay, Gordon and Elinor Collins and George and Diane Cook. All the spouses of the Trust members have been active partners in many, many ways. They have written letters, prayed, hosted missionaries, organised itineraries, opened their homes, brought food and manned the kitchen for AGM dinners or guest speakers. Without support from the spouses the Trust would not have functioned nearly as well as it has, and does.

# The Fourth Decade

1997–2007

### John Moore: Trust member 1975–2006, Chairman 1997–2001

After Ron Paterson stepped down, John Moore was elected to the position of chairman. John and his wife Yvonne first heard about Waidale when they moved from Nelson in 1973 to purchase a farm in the Wendon Valley. He always had a heart for missions and as a young man thought that one day he might go out on the mission field. So they were delighted when they began attending the Waikaka Presbyterian Church and met many of the locals who were involved in Waidale. John loved the concept of the Trust and immediately wanted to be a supporter.

However not everything worked out as they had planned and losing possession of their farm was a devastating blow. But rather than acting as a death knell, the subsequent court ruling led to new and unexpected opportunities. They discovered that when hard things happen God is able to turn them around for good. Betty and Stuart Smith offered them their old family home to rent, resulting in a lifelong friendship. Waidale Trust farmers offered to graze some of their stock until they knew

**Relying on God has to start all over every day, as if nothing has yet been done.**
– C. S. Lewis

what their future would be. John and Yvonne were grateful and continued to manage their stock on each property. The three Moore children loved their visits to Charlie Kerse's farm. His wife, Jeanette, would bring out morning tea including marmite and potato chip sandwiches. They took a great liking to those sandwiches, and they remained a favourite for many years.

John was elected to the Waidale Trust in 1975, the year after they moved to a new property at Moa Flat, and he remained actively involved for thirty-one years. The sixty-kilometre trip to meetings was never an issue. He had a positive attitude: 'If you really want to go somewhere, you just get up and go.' John and Yvonne often hosted missionaries in their home and, since John's death in 2006, Yvonne has continued to maintain contact with them. John was committed to his farming and although he never served in mission overseas, his love for the Lord and interest in missions did not waver. While at Moa Flat he introduced their neighbours, Ken and Jan Robb, to Waidale. They also became supporters and Ken served as a trustee for more than ten years. During the time John and Yvonne lived in the south, the Waidale Trust was an important part of their Christian lives.

At the time John stepped into the chair, the Trust assets were at a comfortable six-figure sum and the 1997 annual report records that in the previous year the Trust had donated $226,837 to support mission.

***

### Flo Brown (nee Hamilton) – International Nepal Fellowship and SIM

Flo first went out to Nepal in 1969, but later spent some time back in New Zealand. Raising support to return overseas again wasn't easy. Her memories are clear:

> I want to say a heart-felt thank you to the Waidale members for your generosity to me both in finance and prayerful concern. I was really struggling to raise my support, having been home for seven years, caring for my mother. As my flight took off and I headed back to Nepal, the words of Isaiah 55:12 came to mind, "You shall go out with joy, and be led forth in peace. The mountains and hills will break into song before you." Yes, God is faithful.

Not only did Flo experience the faithfulness of God for herself, but she was encouraged by the example of those she was serving in Nepal. One occasion she remembers clearly was in the remote village of Ikchung. A group of Christians there had come through much persecution. She was invited to attend the baptisms of five new believers one Saturday morning. Just after daylight they clambered down a cliff to a stream, which they blocked with stones to make it deeper. There, these new believers declared they were putting away idol worship to trust in the Lord Jesus as their Saviour. As she climbed back up the slope, Flo walked with a grandmother who had spent time in jail. The police had told her, "Grandmother, you are too old to go to jail. You might die. Just sign here and we'll let you go." Her reply was, "You can cut my head off, but I won't deny my Lord." Flo was touched by the faith of this dear lady who was a similar age to herself. It was Flo's sixty-third birthday that day so when she was asked to share a few words at the church service which followed, she chose the words of Psalm 63: 'Because You are my help I sing under the shadow of Your wings.'

***

### The Jones Trust

In August 1999 the Waidale Trust took over the Jones Trust. It had been formed in November 1959 by a donation of 4,000 one-pound shares in Leighton Industries Ltd in Auckland. The donors were Mr Frank and Mrs Eva Jones.

The income from half the shares was to be used to support New Zealand missionaries going out with the Bolivian Indian Mission while the remainder was given to other missionary societies as determined by the trustees but including the Methodist Foreign Mission in the Solomon Islands.

Over the years the original investment was sold and reinvested in publicly listed companies. Some of the mission societies that had been supported also changed to become part of larger mission groups. The Bolivian Indian Mission is just one example. The trustees, Mr Eric Lundquist, Mr Robert Wilson and Mr Lindsay Gardiner, who were based in Dunedin, felt unable to continue the work and approached the Waidale Trust to ask if they would accept the responsibility. They saw the Waidale Trust as having similar aims in supporting mission. Waidale agreed and have tried to maintain an interest in New Zealand missionaries working on the South American continent. The new trustees of the Jones Trust nominated from Waidale were Andrew Tripp, Jim Weir (Secretary and Treasurer) and Bruce Heslip (Chairman). The Jones Trust finances are kept separate from those of Waidale.

***

### Deer Farm

At the end of 2000, Waidale had the opportunity to purchase a second property which bordered Gracevale. It was on the open market to be sold by tender and The Waidale Trust was successful. From the beginning it has been leased to Brian Dickison who runs approximately 1,000 stock units, both sheep and deer, on the 223-acre (90.4 ha) property. It is known simply as 'the deer farm', and is quite separate from Gracevale. Capital gains from both of these farms continue to be very good and strengthen the Waidale balance sheet.

***

### Fairlie and Nilanthi Sim

Fairlie first heard about the Waidale Missionary Trust when he worked for John Speden who knew and respected many of the Christian farmers who supported the Trust. Later, while pastoring in Eastern Southland, Fairlie and Nilanthi discovered how much Waidale was a household name in church circles. When God called them to work with SIM in Sudan, the Trust contributed significantly to their support while they served the Khartoum International Church from 2007-2013. They found the generous support was not only financial, but extended to the way in which Trust members took a real personal interest in their journey. Fairlie and Nilanthi knew their newsletters had been read, and they knew they had been upheld in prayer because of the interactive and informed questions they were asked when they came back on home assignment. On their return to New Zealand, SIM NZ asked Fairlie to consider the role of South Island Mobiliser. He accepted, and he and Nilanthi have both been most grateful for Waidale's ongoing support.

Fairlie's role has now grown and, as a couple, they are employed to be responsible for Member Care for the couples and families in SIM NZ. They hope that, God willing, they will return to the

Middle East in the future to serve in a similar role for those Mission Partners (missionaries) who are in other countries.

As their children, Hannah and Daniel, have grown, the Waidale community continues to take an interest in their lives. Fairlie and Nilanthi are continually humbled by the faithfulness of Waidale, not just in getting missionaries to the field but keeping them there through prayer and encouragement, together with genuine caring when they return home. It is a level of support that is not enjoyed to the same extent by all missionaries. They find it is a privilege to partner with the Waidale Missionary Trust, working together to see God's Kingdom come.

1 Corinthians 12:4-6 says:

> There are different kinds of gifts, but the same Spirit distributes them. There are different kinds of service, but the same Lord. There are different kinds of working, but in all of them and in everyone it is the same God at work.

***

## Kenneth and Kim Fleck

In the same year that the Sim family went to Khartoum, Kenneth and Kim Fleck began their mission journey with SIM. Previous involvement in different areas of ministry with the church, Youth for Christ and Scripture Union had begun to prepare them for what lay ahead. Overseas travel fostered a desire to return to engage in mission. Their first step was to move to Auckland with their two young daughters in order to train at the Bible College of New Zealand. God used all of their life experience to grow and equip them for their next challenge, working with people with HIV in Thailand. It captured their imagination, although it was somewhat daunting as they began to learn the language, build relationships with the local people, and understand the needs of a very different culture. They grappled with finding the most effective way of working in an area of ministry that many find just too hard. Over a period of eight years they designed and launched Radical Grace, a ministry focused on being Christ in a broken world. As they partnered with Waidale and with God, to fulfil His vision for mission, they felt privileged.

Kenneth and Kim returned home in 2015, and found it difficult to resettle here. Yet, even in that, they felt supported by the prayers and words of wisdom from people in Waidale. The ministry of Radical Grace has continued and is now led by Daeng and Ann Dechaboon. When Daeng and Ann came to Invercargill in 2017 to speak about their work, a group of Waidale trustees travelled to hear them speak, which was greatly encouraging for the Flecks. Kenneth and Kim conclude:

> Waidale Trust you are impacting the world. When it comes to HIV, many walk by as it is too hard. Thank you for believing in the Flecks and the SIM project Radical Grace.

***

### George Cook: Trust member 1999-, Chairman 2001-2008

George Cook was brought up by parents who were keenly mission-minded. As a young man in 1963 he went on a short-term mission trip with a Bible Class work party to the New Hebrides (now Vanuatu). Back at home, managing the family farm of 700 acres (283.2 ha) fitted around his involvement in Sunday School, Youth Group, Boys' Brigade and Camp Columba. He was an elder at the Waikoikoi Church, a lay preacher and at different times held positions as session clerk and clerk for Presbytery. He served as chairman of the local School committee and was elected to continue in the role after it became the board of trustees. George chaired the Camp Columba committee for a number of years and spent countless hours as one of a team of volunteers who helped with the construction of the camp buildings. He served on the committee which planned camps at Easter and Labour Weekend and he wrote a book telling the full history of the camp at the time of its 50th Jubilee in 2007. After more than ten years of grazing stock for Waidale, he became a trustee in 1999 and a couple of years later he accepted the position of chairman.

One of the last events George chaired before stepping down from the position was the fortieth anniversary celebrations.

A minute of appreciation was recorded:

> George has been a very efficient and faithful chairman. His spiritual insight, evident in the messages he brought to the meetings … has helped to continue the spirit of unity, of purpose and fellowship which has been a feature of the Trust since its formation.

**Fortieth Anniversary**
28 April 2007

Venue: Riversdale Presbyterian Church and Community Centre. Graeme Gardyne, together with Rev John Gullick, conducted the church service.

- The Rev Dr Alan Kerr preached from 2 Corinthians 4:7, reminding those present that God's treasure is held in earthen vessels. A few days prior to the celebration, many had attended James White's funeral service. He was born in the same year that the Trust was established. Although his body became very frail and weak from muscular dystrophy, the light of the gospel shone brightly from his life.
- Chairman George Cook welcomed more than 100 people who were supporters of the Trust or who had been supported by the Trust to the celebratory dinner. A flower posy was presented to Elinor Collins in recognition of her nineteen years serving as secretary of the Trust. An item by John, Catherine and Ben Mwangi of Kenya was well received.
- Speakers Andrew and Margaret Dunn shared their experience from a recent visit to the Kapuna district in Papua New Guinea and the United Church of New Guinea congregation in Port Moresby. A poignant moment for them was visiting the grave of their young son Robert.

- Averil Bennett (nee McIntosh) looked back over forty years of change in mission. She and her husband Alan had seen many changes in Thailand as nationals began to take responsibility for their churches. Partnering in nationwide networks helped the church to grow. Likewise, the Waidale Missionary Trust needed to build in a way that would secure its future and continue the mission vision of its founders.
- Margery White and her son Richard cut the cake. Chairman George Cook acknowledged their significant family contribution to the Trust, together with founding trustees, Ron Paterson, Clarence Gardyne and George Simpson.
- Chris Cowie, recently retired director of SIM NZ, brought greetings from newly appointed director Nigel Webb and from missionaries Jim and Diane Young and Maree Scully. He expressed gratitude for generous monetary and prayer support, from Waidale, for their missionaries over many years. He acknowledged the importance of Waidale support, which helped to enlarge their vision for growth in the Kingdom of God.

A vote of thanks from Hamish Mackay, prayer and singing the doxology concluded the evening.

*Top: Re-enactment of the perceived conversation between Harry White and Clarence Gardyne as presented by Malcolm White and John Gardyne at the 50th Jubilee celebration. Bottom: Cutting of the cake by Ron Paterson, Margaret Gardyne and Dulcie Paterson.*

*Top: Margery White, second from left, with Richard, Mary-Anne, Malcolm and Rob. Inset: James White. Bottom: Margaret Gardyne with Graeme, Helen, Jane and John at the 50th Jubilee celebrations.*

*Top: John Gardyne shows trustees around Gracevale and the deer farm during a visit in 2017. Bottom: Future generations. Hayden Gardyne with his grandad Graeme Gardyne loading out lambs for Waidale.*

*Top: Rob Reynolds, NZ director of SIM, speaking at the Jubilee dinner.*
*Bottom: Maree Scully, speaking of her work in South Asia.*

*Top: Kim and Kenneth Fleck who launched Radical Grace ministry in Thailand. Bottom: Scripture Union representatives at the dinner: Aaron Douglas with Nigel and Hannah Winder.*

*Top: James Allaway of TSCF.*
*Bottom: Phil McCallum speaks at the dinner about the future of Waidale.*

*General view of the 50th Jubilee dinner.*

*Trustees 2017. Back Row: Hamish Mackay, Miriam Mackay, Diane Cook (Secretary), Phil McCallum, John Gardyne, Jonathan Gardyne, David Smith, Robert Erskine, Doug Dodds, Richard White, Peter Gardyne. Front Row: George Cook, Elinor Collins, Graeme Gardyne (Chairman), Betty Smith, Jim Weir. Absent: Bruce Roy, James Roy, Jeremy McPhail, Andrew Tripp, John Wilson.*

# The Fifth Decade

2007–2017

Each decade has brought new challenges for the Trust. As the number of applications for funding has increased, the criteria had to be reviewed.

## Anna Boyd (nee McKee)

Anna had spent time on a Mercy Ship as well as nursing in both Benin and Sierra Leone. She applied to the Trust before she began working with Maternity Africa in June 2014. Working in a hospital, managing health for the poorest women in Tanzania and Ethiopia is a big task. Anna reflects on her journey:

> Being the first girl in my family for 60 years, my father didn't quite know what to make of such a small human. He fed me up on tonics, oils and supplements, but alas, I never grew much more than five feet. It seems God had plans for me to work with other small people. As a nurse He has led me to different parts of Africa to work with women with terrible birth injuries, caused because their pelvis is too small and they do not get the medical help they need. I would tower over these tiny women, who would fit neatly under my arm. They were tiny in stature

> but giants in terms of personality. They have taught me so much about resilience, persistence in the face of adversity, and what God's love can do through all people – big and small. No one is forgotten to Him. My journey has been made possible with the support of Waidale and I look forward to continuing in Tanzania for as long as God leads me.

At the beginning of the fifth decade there was another change of Waidale Trust office-bearers. Doug Dodds was elected to replace George Cook as chairman. Diane Cook accepted nomination as secretary. The Cooks had already retired to Gore and now their home became the venue for Trust meetings. With the Jubilee approaching it would be a busy time.

***

### Diane Cook: Secretary 2008–

Diane was born and brought up in Gore, but her grandparents lived next door to the Wybers at Clydevale. The two families knew each other well so when Margaret Currie (nee Wyber) first went to Sarawak as a missionary, Diane's mission interest was awakened. After she and George married, they lived and farmed at Waikoikoi. She became aware of Waidale when George first grazed stock for the Trust, but it wasn't until some time later she became fully aware of its significance. She was involved in Gore Tel-A-Story, a mission to local children founded by Child Evangelisation Fellowship. It was supported by Waidale. Children could make a phone call to hear a pre-recorded story with a Christian message and they could attend special activity programmes. The organisation always entered a float in the local Christmas parade. When Diane was asked to speak about Tel-A-Story at a Waidale Trust function at

Dunrobin church, she felt very nervous. For the following few years, Tel-A-Story hosted a programme for the children at the Trust AGM. When Diane was approached and asked to consider taking on the role of Trust secretary, she was aware it was a big job, and knew she had big shoes to fill following the sterling service Elinor had given. Certainly she was qualified for the job. She had worked in administrative jobs before marriage. Over the years she had been secretary for Presbyterial and for Plunket. The 50th Jubilee celebrations were a huge undertaking. Yet she has grown in the role. She and George have hosted many missionaries in their home, giving invaluable personal contact. It confirmed to them the paramount importance of communication. The advent of internet banking and email correspondence has brought changes. There are advantages because urgent prayer requests from missionaries can be forwarded to Trust members quickly. Praying for missionaries at each meeting certainly maintains a personal profile, that she believes is important.

She enjoys writing letters to missionaries at the time cheques are sent. And when those cheques are sent by regular mail, receipts are required, which is a tangible way of knowing the money has arrived at its destination. She hopes that Waidale will not become a faceless organisation because of technology.

Younger Trust members now bring mobiles or tablets to meetings rather than notes or pens. It certainly saves paper. The guff sheet, started by Elinor Collins, has become the Waidale News, and when printed may equal up to ten sides of A3 size paper. The recent decision to appoint a minute secretary has made her job as correspondence secretary much easier. She reflects:

> I have been truly blessed with all the wonderful people that have come into my life since becoming the Secretary of The Waidale Missionary Trust. The trustees, graziers, missionaries, people we supported and supporters of the Trust have all helped

me to have a deeper love and appreciation of every person that God has called to mission work, both overseas and in New Zealand. I thought the position would have been far beyond my capabilities but I believe that God called me to do it and then proceeded to give me the enabling. I also could not have done it without the help and support of my dear husband, George – to God be the Glory.

***

## Tertiary Students Christian Fellowship (TSCF) and Student Life

Some of the current Waidale Trust members have been active in TSCF or Student Life. Both organisations have an important spiritual influence on the lives of students within our universities and tertiary campuses. New Zealand is now regarded as a secular nation and so these are vital places in which to share the gospel among those who have the opportunity to rise to positions of influence in places of business and authority.

Garth is one of those people. He was raised in a single parent household before he went to Dunedin to study. When he met up with a Student Life worker he was keen to talk about God and about faith and over successive weeks and months he asked questions, read books, went on camp and eventually reached a point where he made a commitment to Christ. He has continued to grow and mature and became an active member of Student Life, keen to share the good news with other students.

**This generation of Christians is responsible for this generation of souls on the earth.**
– Keith Green

A recent university graduate, also from Southland and also named Garth, attributes his growth in the Christian faith to his involvement with TSCF. He tells his story:

> God has taken me on a great adventure from when I first joined Christian Fellowship. [CF]. Today I look back knowing I've grown substantially in my faith, and also managed to get a cheeky wee degree on the side.
>
> At Lincoln I've accomplished many tremendous feats, including serving hundreds of snags (sausages), heaps of toasties and a few southern cheese rolls too. The friends I've made at CF will be friends for life. Bonding with people over a mutual faith in Jesus creates a friendship deeper than any other. Bible studies have often been the backbone of my Christian walk on campus, a mid-week stability to help keep me on the path. Co-leading them last year firstly forced me to be more organised and has also shown me how much I have to learn about the one book which life pivots around.
>
> Mission on campus was the biggest challenge for me, being seen by my uni mates as "one of those Christians." As time went on those same friends complimented me on staying true to what I believe and not stooping to stuff they now regret. I'd like to thank CF for always being a great community with great uplifting biblical chat. CF at Lincoln and my friends there have steered me in the right direction and helped me develop into the man I am today – certainly not perfect but following the narrow path where the Lord leads.

***

### Doug Dodds: Trust member 1998-, Chairman 2008-2016

When Doug Dodds was studying for a degree in Agricultural

Science at Lincoln College, he was involved with Lincoln College Christian Fellowship and served as president for one year. He had no inkling of how this would help to shape his life for his future involvement with Waidale.

He is a third generation dairy farmer on 'Middlevale' at Charlton, south of Gore. With his wife, Josephine, they milk 460 cows while additional heifers and bulls are raised for sale or lease.

After returning home from Lincoln he became actively involved in the Mataura Presbyterian Church, where he served on session and also as chairman of the Deacons' court. His interest in mission was first triggered through Ben and Elspeth Kong, who worked in the church prior to their going to Thailand with OMF.

His involvement with Waidale began after he had attended the funeral of Harry White. The testimony of Harry's life and the way in which he and others were able to use their farms to support missionary work impacted Doug. He saw an opportunity to contribute so he phoned Graeme Gardyne. He offered to raise bull calves he had bred through to slaughter at two years old rather than having Waidale purchase stock for him to graze, because bringing in stock from outside posed a risk of disease transfer to his dairy herd. The offer was accepted and led to him being invited to become a trustee. Later he was elected as the fourth chairman of the Trust. His involvement has greatly enlarged his knowledge and appreciation of mission. He reflects:

> During my time as Chairman, we sought to codify which people and projects we would support, so as not to spread our efforts too thinly, and to be able to keep a prayerful interest in all whom we supported financially. To a large extent, however, the Trust continued to uphold the vision of its founders, and did so in a harmonious and cheerful manner.

One of those founders, Clarence Gardyne, passed away in 2016. His widow, Margaret, treasures the minute of appreciation that was presented to him on his retirement from the Trust in 2014. It epitomises his character:

> The Board of Trustees of the Waidale Missionary Trust wish to record their deep appreciation and give thanks to God for the long service Clarence Gardyne has given to the ministry of the gospel of the Lord Jesus Christ through the Trust. He has been a member of the Board since its inception following a public meeting on June 5th 1967, called by those who wanted to help the Rev Andrew Dunn finance his proposed missionary assignment in Papua New Guinea … Over the passage of time Clarence has gained a wide knowledge of the missionary challenge both overseas and in New Zealand … Clarence's wise counsel has encouraged us all very much and has always been of benefit to the decisions made at Trust meetings.

Although Clarence was not there for the jubilee, what a thrill it must have been for him to have known that his sons, a son-in-law and two grandsons were serving on the Trust.

***

### Fiftieth Jubilee

It was most fitting that Graeme Gardyne had the privilege of leading the Trust into the 50th Jubilee celebrations held at Calvin Community Church in Gore on 1 July 2017. The occasion was a momentous milestone in the history of Waidale.

During the afternoon a large number of attendees shared in afternoon tea at a meet-and-greet held at Camp Columba at Pukerau near Gore. Waidale Trust support for ministry at Camp Columba has been an integral part of its development. A number of the Trust members worked to establish the campsite long before Waidale was formed, and they have continued to have a vested interest in the growing ministry there. Some of the missionaries supported by Waidale remember it as the place where they first felt called by God, and they have returned to speak at youth camps held there over Easter and Labour Weekends. Ritchie and Dirkje Kelly were managers at Camp Columba for twenty-two years. They wholeheartedly supported the Waidale Trust. Dirkje served as a trustee for ten years.

Camp Columba has been developed and enlarged beyond expectation. Its reputation in the Southland community is impressive. Regular school holiday camps are very popular.

On its website it describes its mission: To demonstrate God's love to all who come to Camp.

For the evening jubilee programme, more than 200 people from throughout New Zealand, and from Australia, gathered to celebrate and to give thanks to God. Among them was Andrew Dunn, who was gratified to be there with two of his daughters, Cathy and Karen. Sadly Margaret had passed away a few months earlier. He brought a greeting recalling God's call to mission overseas when he was fifteen years of age.

At Calvin Church, various missions set up displays in the foyer area featuring their work. When the official proceedings began in the auditorium a small orchestra led the worship beginning with the hymn, Great is Thy Faithfulness. It was a fitting way to start the evening. Averil Bennett said grace and between courses of the catered meal, there were guest speakers and tributes were given to those who had established the Trust. Two of the original trustees, Ron Paterson and George Simpson, were present. George led the gathering in prayer, while Ron, his wife Dulcie and Margaret Gardyne cut the cake.

**Rob Reynolds**, New Zealand director of SIM, spoke of the sense of partnership and community fostered over many years between Waidale and SIM, as they continue to work together towards the same goal. In 2017 seventeen of their forty-seven New Zealand missionaries were receiving support from Waidale. For those missionaries, it is so much more than financial support: it is an investment in people through prayer and sharing news. In a world where change is needed to keep the church relevant and vibrant, Rob believes it is important to realise that although methods and mission need to adapt, principles do not change. He compared Waidale's sense of mission to the example of Gaius, in 3 John, who showed faithfulness towards the truth, realised the importance of sharing the journey in community and chose to be part of what God was doing. Rob concluded that Waidale can face the future with eagerness as the result of investing in mission, based on those same principles.

**Maree Scully**, who has spent fourteen years in South Asia with SIM, spoke of her work there among many first-generation Christians. In the same way that people have invested in her life, she feels privileged to have an opportunity to invest into the lives of young believers and watch God growing them in their faith. She has learnt that in God's economy nothing is wasted, and she loves passing on the things she has learnt such as wise stewardship of resources, pastoral care and management, and training for leadership. As a new missionary she experienced first-hand the difficulties of leaving behind the familiar support network of friends and family but throughout her time away the support, encouragement and prayer of Waidale members has been a vital part of her journey.

**Martin Campbell** of WEC referred to the beautiful Gracevale farm, nestled in the Wendon Valley with a view towards the hills, and cautioned that life is not all about the valley. It is easy to put our feet up there, but it is important to keep looking over the hill, to be concerned for those out of sight on the other side who may not have heard of Jesus and His light and salvation. Even in mission it is easy to become anaesthetised, and people can become self-centred without realising it. When Jonah reneged on his Nineveh assignment, God promptly reminded him, 'Should I not be concerned about the people of Nineveh?' We too must never lose sight of the fact that God is at work and He wants people to know that He cares. Martin put out a challenge to keep the vision alive, because settling into maintenance mode brings death, not life.

***

## The Future

One of the newer, younger Trust members, Philip (Phil) McCallum, spoke of the future of the Trust. Phil, with his wife Katherine, farm a mix of sheep, dairy support and run an Angus beef stud on their property in the Balfour area. His first association with the Waidale Trust was through his father-in-law, John Wilson, then a trustee, who ran cattle for Waidale. He asked Phil if he would run 20 ewes for Camp Columba.

One of the biggest challenges Phil has found as a new trustee is getting his head around all the individuals, ministries and organisations the Trust supports. As his understanding has grown, he has been interested to follow the journeys of the different missionaries. Relationships with people and supporters of Waidale keep Phil engaged and passionate about the Trust, and encourage him to build on what has already been accomplished.

He has seen the financial diversity that the Trust has developed in the past 50 years with income streams derived from sheep and beef trading, as well as shares, loans and bonds. Phil believes that this needs to continue into the future and that the Trust will be open to innovative ideas. New trustees will help to bring different perspectives and skills to the working of the Trust.

He shared his reflections and his vision:

> From small beginnings 50 years ago, a few farmers from the Knapdale-Waikaka Riversdale and Waikaia areas had a vision. They had a desire to help one family – the Dunns – to raise funds so they could get to the mission field.
>
> A Trust was formed. It was originally called the Waidale Charitable Trust but was soon changed to The Waidale Missionary Trust.
>
> Waidale has now grown by God's grace and helps many people fulfil the call of God to minister in New Zealand and all over the world.
>
> That first year the Trust gave a total of $4,000. Now, 50 years later, the 2016 figure was $252, 087. The previous year, 2015, it was $271,320.
>
> Over the 50 years an estimated $5.75 million has been given, consisting of $1.25 million given in the first 25 years and $4.5 million given in the last 25 years.
>
> In those early years the income was derived from selling sheep and cattle. Now Waidale has a portfolio of investments which involves:
>
> – sheep and cattle
> – two farms which are leased
> – shares (known as the Jones Trust, established 1999)
> – commercial loans
> – bonds
> – donations
>
> Income structure is an ever-changing area as new ideas to help

grow, diversify and protect the funds of the Waidale Missionary Trust for the future are always welcome.

The Trust has around 35 farmers who graze stock: ewes and lambs, cows and calves, steers or heifers. In 2016, 193 cattle and 560 lambs were processed; and in 2015, 178 cattle and 747 lambs were processed.

With God's grace the Waidale Missionary Trust has now grown its assets to $4.8 million of accumulated funds that can be used to glorify God.

The Trust has 55 past and present trustees with two more accepting the call to start this year.

Out of the total of 57 trustees there are two founding members who have representatives on the Trust from three generations. There is also one missionary family who has had three generations supported by the Trust: the McIntoshes, the Bennetts and now the Tippers.

The Trust has supported one missionary for 39 years, and that person is still being supported on the mission field today. Gore Counselling and IHC have been supported long-term by the trust.

These are some of the highlights of the last 50 years. We give thanks to God for the ability to use these funds to glorify him. We are also very thankful for trustees, graziers, missionaries and others who put their faith in God and the Waidale Missionary Trust and helped shape what it is today.

Graeme Gardyne, in his closing comments, said that he remains continually inspired by his own father, Clarence, who never lost his enthusiasm even when he was an old man. He challenged supporters to rekindle the vision and enthusiasm imparted by those who had established the Trust through prayer, mutual encouragement and unity of purpose. He recalled the message given by

Norman McIntosh at the tenth anniversary to be audacious for God and to keep our eyes fixed on Jesus, rather than on the winds of changing circumstances. Graeme acknowledged that because the face of farming in the twenty-first century is very different, new ways of generating income is necessary and attracting younger supporters, both as graziers and as trust members, is pivotal to the future of Waidale. His annual report written a few weeks later concluded with the words of Paul. They epitomise fifty years of sacrificial giving by many faithful men and women of God who have been part of The Waidale Missionary Trust.

> Let us not become weary in doing good, for at the proper time we will reap a harvest if we do not give up. Therefore, as we have opportunity, let us do good to all people, especially to the family of believers (Galatians 6:9-10).

# Appendix

## A Selection of Messages Received at the Time of the Fiftieth Jubilee

Congratulations for fifty years of serving our Lord and making a huge difference for countless lives. Thank you for helping to make it possible for our missionaries and mission to achieve what we would not be able to do without your partnership. – **Owen Brown, National Director, One Mission Society**

Congratulations on celebrating your 50th Jubilee. Thank you so much for your support and encouragement. – **International Needs**

Dear Waidale friends, we are so excited that you have reached this massive milestone. Congratulations on 50 faithful years of mission service. The hope, vision and faith which began this Trust has seen more people come to know Jesus, be healed, be taught and be provided for, so many more than was probably imagined. The eternal impact of your commitment will only be truly known when you stand before the King of Kings. Thank you from the bottom of our hearts. – **Rochelle and Nigel Webb, former director SIM NZ, now serving in Colombia**

The Waidale Missionary Trust has generously supported our work over a number of years which has enabled it to continue and to flourish. We are enormously grateful for their generosity in this way. We see our work as part of the mission of the Church and of the Gospel, reaching students and staff in the name of Christ. We give thanks to God for those who set up the Waidale Missionary Trust and who have continued this great work for 50 years. May God continue to bless all you do. – **Professor Paul Trebilco, Otago Tertiary Chaplaincy Trust Board**[14]

Our grateful thanks to the Waidale Trust folk for their wonderful support and prayers over our sixteen years in Japan. We trust that they will be able to continue their good work in supporting missionaries as they serve the Lord. – **John and Lesley Holden, formerly with One Mission Society**

Without your prayer and support would our four girls all be walking with the Lord now? Would we have been able to maintain financial support levels and buy a suitable vehicle for our time in Burkina Faso? Would we have had a strong support network to come home to in times of trouble? To all these and many more challenges the answer would most surely be, 'Without Waidale – No!' Our interaction over the years has been nothing but a major blessing to all our family, let alone the countless Fulani that have greatly benefitted in both this life and their coming eternal life via Waidale support. – **Jim and Helen Harrington, SIM**

Your belief in us has given hope to us and those we work directly

---

14. The board employs two full-time chaplains in Dunedin at the University of Otago and the Otago Polytechnic as well as voluntary assistants, serving around 25,000 students and 5,000 staff.

with in Thailand. Thank you so much for your vision and generosity and faithfulness. – **Kenneth and Kim Fleck, SIM**

Thank you for your support to us as a family and being part of God's ministry to the Sisaala people in Ghana. – **Dave and Helen Dunn, SIM**

Thank you for your continued support of Camp Columba and the many lives that have been touched by prayer, finances and your encouragement. – **Andrew and Sarah Currie, Easter Camp committee (now Christian Youth Events committee)**

I have watched Waidale Trust from conception and I pay tribute to those who had the vision to launch it. God has blessed it greatly. – **Ivan Elder**

We are thankful for your partnership and your investment over several years as we continue to reach students for Christ, change students for life and grow a new generation of Christian leaders. The vision and innovation of the Trust is inspirational to many across all of New Zealand. Your generous grants have been a large part of seeing men and women – both New Zealanders and many international students – meet Jesus in our New Zealand tertiary institutes. Thank you. – **TSCF, Tertiary Students Christian Fellowship**

Well done Waidale! It's a real privilege to be part of an awesome team. Long may this ministry continue. – **Mark and Louise Heslip, Graziers**

What a wonderful evening of inspiration … I am so very grateful for the support and encouragement of the Waidale Trust both for CEF and myself, especially when I left CEF. The ministry God gave me among the children and families in Levin is growing, thanks to the Trust. I will always appreciate the vision God gave the men who initiated this wonderful ministry of support. – **Pam Brooking, Former director of Child Evangelism Fellowship**

Thank you for inviting me on behalf of Gore IHC to be with you as you celebrated the 50th anniversary of the Waidale Trust. I enjoyed the evening immensely … the meal, the excellent speakers and the warmth of the 200 good-natured attendees present, made for a very special occasion which I was so privileged to be a part of. I had not realised that your trust was so large and so successful in what it set out to achieve … I thank your trustees for their thoughtfulness and generosity and for the wonderful support you have given to the Gore branch of IHC over so many years. – **Jim Tattersfield, IHC**

Congratulations to the Waidale Missionary Trust on their 50th celebrations. The abundant fruit that has been evident throughout the years is testimony to the faithfulness of the Trust's commitment to prayer, mission and their heart towards God. As part of the generation that is now picking up the baton of ministry, we are inspired and challenged by the Waidale story to have a similar pioneering spirit not just for our generation, but for the generations to come. Thank you for your faithfulness and your commitment to the spread of the gospel; we pray for an even stronger and more fruitful impact for the next fifty years. – **Rev Marty and Steph Redhead, Christchurch**

I want to take this opportunity to say a massive thank you for the support I have received from the Waidale Trust. I would not have survived without the generous donations that came to me over the last five years … Once in India when I was feeling overwhelmed by the sheer volume of need, God reminded me that He only required me to be like one drop of water of obedience and for me to leave the ripple effect to him. Can you imagine how many drops of water the Waidale Trust has been, not just in the lives of the people they are supporting but also through the ripple effect of each one of those drops. That picture in my mind is truly amazing. It is so how God works, using different parts of His body for different tasks. – **Ann Weatherburn, formerly with Pioneers**

Many thanks to the Waidale Trust for 50 years of faithful support to God's work around the world. May God bring a 100-fold increase of spiritual fruit from your investment of love, sacrifice and generosity. – **Maree Scully, SIM, Southeast Asia**

This work is clearly one the Lord started, blessed and provided for. And the Lord is using it to send salt and light into the world. May He continue to use you and sustain the vision for the next 50 years, or until the Lord returns! – **Martin Campbell, Eastwest College, Gordonton**

Please pass on my gratitude to the trustees of Waidale for their faithful support of Scripture Union NZ over so many years. The legacy that The Waidale Missionary Trust has created is impressive and the kingdom is far better off for the generosity and vision of the trustees, past and present. Scripture Union NZ has benefitted mightily and we are grateful for the support that has enabled staff to get on with their jobs of teaching the gospel to children and young people. – **Wayne Fraser, National Director Scripture Union NZ**

Congratulations Waidale Trust on 50 years of supporting our God's great commission. We thank you that you have been a redwood tree to so many people helping them to do what God has called them to. Thank you for your support for us. – **Rob and Katherine Barr, SIM mission partners designate to West Africa**

The Lord has abundantly multiplied the act of faith of the original trustees and those who have joined them over the years. Heaven alone will reveal the full story of people who have been won for Christ and discipled overseas, and here at home, through the support you have given His servants … May the Lord continue to bless the work of the Trust in the future. It is playing a vital role in God's work. – **Allan and Maureen Goulstone, Navigators NZ**

May you each be encouraged as you faithfully enable and participate in what God is doing in all corners of the world. – **Daniel and Anita Muir, SIM Zambia**

We have been receiving financial support for our work in Pakistan from The Waidale Missionary Trust since 2012. When we first heard about Waidale we were amazed that a group of Kiwi farmers would be so innovative in their fundraising efforts. What a great idea! And then we found out just how generous Waidale has been over the years, and continues to be. Millions of dollars have been given to a great variety of ministries that are working to fulfil the Great Commission. Thank you for including us in this great tradition. We feel like we are part of something special. – **Allen and Elizabeth O'Loughlin, Bach Christian Hospital, Pakistan**

Greetings, and congratulations on the occasion of your 50th anniversary. Your efforts and dedication have been blessed by God as through the years you have been enabled to support the work and ministry of missions and church growth. – **Alistair Perkins, Far East Broadcasting**

We pass on our congratulations to the Waidale Trust for 50 years of faithful service to God's work through missions at home and abroad. We pray it will be a very special time as people give thanks to the faithfulness of God and the faithfulness of the farmers of Southland in giving generously over all these years to God's work. We will be praying and celebrating with you all the way from Malawi. – **Jim and Diane Young, SIM**

The vision that started the work of the Trust 50 years ago has developed into a unique ministry that is impacting lives both here in New Zealand and around the world. Helen and I are very grateful for the generous way you have supported us in prayer and with finances during our forty-two years of ministry with SIM. We will never forget our partnership with you in our ministry in Benin, here in the SIM New Zealand office, and most recently in Nigeria. Thank you for the way you welcomed us and cared for us during our home assignments. We know that the Waidale Trust's significant role will continue into the future. May God give you much wisdom as you develop your strategic service for Him in the years to come. It is our prayer that God will encourage you all as you serve Him.

May the God of hope fill you with all joy and peace as you trust in Him, so that you may overflow with hope by the power of the Holy Spirit (Romans 15:13). – **Chris and Helen Cowie, SIM**

Sorry Gordon and Roswitha weren't able to make it as they are overseas, but we praise God for Waidale's support for them and for Jo and Kristie. Two generations of support since 1977. – **Johann Bayne**

***

## A Cross Section of People and Organisations Supported 1967–2017

**AEM (Andes Evangelical Mission, formerly BIM – Bolivian Indian Mission)**: Ken and Dorothy Holroyd, Elspeth and Bruce Anderson

**Africa Evangelical Fellowship**: Ngaire Reid

**AIM (Africa Inland Mission)**: Ben and Winsome Webster, Dr Andrew Hill, Russell and Mireille Cross, Johan and David Gladstone, Christine and Bruce Turner

**Anne Bowie**, Presbyterian Church

**Asia Theological Research & Development NZ Trust**: Bruce Nicholls

**Asian Outreach:** Margaret Currie

**Bible College of NZ**: Andrew Gardyne, Ruth Howe, Heather Clark, Bruce Allan, Karl and Lynley Lamb, Andrew Tripp, Mark and Anna Winter, David Smaill

**Bible Society**

**Boys' Brigade NZ**

**Camp Columba, Pukerau**

**Chaplaincy in Schools**: Gore, Calvin Community Church

**Child Evangelism Fellowship**: Otago-Southland Good News Clubs, Gore Tel-A-Story and camps, Pam Brooking

**Christian Broadcasting Association**

**Christian Resource Centre**

**Christian Youth Events Committee**: Easter and Labour Weekend Camps

**Church of Christ Mission School**: Janet McKinlay (Hong Kong)

**Churches Education Commission**: Christian Religious Education (Bible in Schools)

**CYC (Christian Youth Camps) Waihola**

**Delta Community Trust**: Pastor

**Dunedin Christian School**: Liberton

**Empower Asia**: Paul Somerville

**Every Nations Ministries**: Andre Lietze, Paul and Tanya Jack

**Far East Broadcasting Corporation**: Staff support in New Zealand

**Focus on the Family**

**Girls' Brigade NZ**: Fonomarae

**Global Connections in Mission**: Johan Gladstone

**Gore Counselling Service**

**Harvest Partnership**: Ken Rout

**Health Songs International**: Rob Greaney

**IHC Gore Committee**

**Independent**: Johann and Kristie Bayne, Gordon and Roswitha Bayne (Benin)

**Inter-Varsity Fellowship**

**International Needs**: Ray Harrison, Jeremy Denmead, Gradon Harvey.

**Interserve – (formerly Bible and Medical Missionary Fellowship or BMMF)**: Scott Dumbleton, Roelant and Rosemary Dewerse, Alan and Shirley Ferguson, Gavin and Jenny McIntosh, Berys Miller, A Thomson, Hugh Kemp, Peter and Kerryn Christensen, Allen and Elizabeth O'Loughlin, Dennis Fountain, Beulah Wood, Alan and Beth Simpson

**Keswick Pounawea Convention**

**Lay Institute for Evangelism**: Doug Malcolm

**Living Springs, Christchurch**

**Ludhiana Hospital, India**

**Missionary Aviation Fellowship**: Bill and Angela Harding (Jones Trust), Melissa Laird

**Navigators NZ**: Mike and Audrey Shamy, Jonathon and Fernah Peacey, Peter and Margaret Bramley, Sandy and Judy Fairservice, Allan and Maureen Goulstone

**OAC (Open Air Campaigners)**: Bob McNaughton, Michael and Audrey Shaskey, Ivan Grindlay

**OMF**: Norman and Amy McIntosh, Elsie McDonald, Keith and Linnet Hinton, Bryan and Iona (Twink) Parry, Heather Calder, Averil and Alan Bennett, Brydon Bennett, Callum and Fiona McKinlay, Ben and Elspeth Kong, Margaret and David Brown, Warren and Doreen Payne, New Zealand Director support.

**OMS (One Mission Society NZ)**: Lesley and John Holden, Dennis Shuker, Owen and Avalon Brown, Chunillal Pema, Mark and Anne Pavelka, Jean Woods

**Operation Mercy**: John and Kristina Tipper

**Otago Tertiary Chaplaincy**: Paul Trebilco

**Pioneers**: Jennifer Thompson, Ann Weatherburn,

**Presbyterian Church Overseas Mission**: Andrew and Margaret Dunn

**Prison Fellowship**: in New Zealand and Margaret Currie (Mongolia)

**PSSA (Presbyterian Social Services Assn.) Resthaven, Gore**

**Radio Rhema – Rhema Media**: Maree Simpson, and general support

**Save the Family Crusade**: Bob Kingi

**Scripture Union NZ**: Jill Fleck, Nigel Winder, Ben Necklen, Aaron Douglas, Paul Humphreys, Ben Febery, Josephine McEwing, Bronwyn McKenzie, Jane Troughton, Helen Martin, Brenton Hackfath, Bruce Conway

**Servants to Asia's Urban Poor**: Colin and Janet Harrington, Dave and Kerry Verkade

**SIM**: Gordon and Roswitha Bayne, Chris and Helen Cowie, Janet Winch, Doug and Nelly Allen, Murray and Pam Dunn, Bruce and Noreen Bond, Richard and Annette Edlin, Jim and Helen Harrington, K and J Brown, Stephen and Rachel Thompson, Nathan and Debra Wilson, Andrew Brown, Flo Hamilton, Sarah Kerr, Andrew Gardyne, Murray and Alison Ure, Helen and David Dunn, Daniel and Anita Muir, Derek Birks, Pete and Christine Johnstone, Jim and Diane Young, Maree Scully, Andrew and Elizabeth Buxton, Carl and Sharlene Pilkington, Fairlie and Nilanthi Sim, Malcolm and Rebecca Pirie, Kenneth and Kim Fleck, Andrew and Kate Ure, Merle Ashworth, Paula McFarlane, John and Jackie Paine, Nigel and Richelle Webb, Kingsley and Marie Morris, Katherine and Rob Barr

**Spiritual Growth Ministries**: Andrew and Margaret Dunn

**Sports Chaplaincy Southland**: Shane and Sarah Auld

**St James Church, South Dunedin**: Gordon and Joan Homer

**Straight Up Trust**: Rock Solid: Debbie and Graham Henderson, Joshua Bruce, Ollie Yeoman, Marina Conway, Olivia Hall, James Roy

**Student Life**: Mikey Chen, Jandre and Michaela Niehaus, Bonnie and Aidan Shotbolt, Steve and Lilee Checketts

**Student Soul, Dunedin**

**TEAR Fund**

**Tertiary Students Christian Fellowship**: Gavin McIntosh, Mike Simpson, James Allaway, Paul Somerville

**The Parenting Place**: John Cowan and Attitude programme

**Tranzsend**: Joanna Redhead

**Turakina Maori Girls' School**

**Waimea Christian Trust**: The Hub, Riversdale.

**WEC**: Colin and Janet Harrington, Geof and Shiron Nicholson, Ross and Avrille Campbell, David and Jacqui Hammond, John and Elizabeth McDonald, Andrew and Jan Bovey, Martin and Joyce Campbell, Joseph and Lois Bateson

**Word of Life**: David and Ainsley Gow

**Wycliffe Bible Translators**: Bruce and Carol Symons, Chris Cullen

**YFC** (Youth for Christ): Ian Grant, Jim Gilchrist, Y-One, Vaughan Fenton, Dean and T. Comerford, Karen McCauley, Peter and Emma Scarlet

**Youth with a Mission**: Jim and Allison Wescombe, David and Susan Cole, Gabrielle and Simon Pooley, Laura Coppin

***

## Trust Members

| | |
|---|---|
| Ron Paterson | 1967–2010 |
| Clarence Gardyne | 1967–2014 |
| Harry White | 1967–1990 |
| George Simpson | 1967–2014 |
| Bert Gardyne | 1967–1979 |
| Pearson Johnston | 1967–1976 |
| Lewis Mackay | 1967–1987 |
| Bruce Wilson | 1967–1981 |
| Margery White | 1967–2013 |
| Pamela Davies | 1967–1969 |
| Stan Clark | 1967–1995 |
| Don Tayles | 1967–2006 |
| Jack Hansen | 1967–1970 |
| Betty Smith | 1969 – |
| Bruce McLay | 1970–1972 |
| Cliff Clark | 1971–1997 |
| Alister Keown | 1971–1976 |

| | |
|---|---|
| Jim McNamara | 1974–1981 |
| Ernie Goodwin | 1975–1982 |
| John Moore | 1975–2006 |
| Keith Halliday | 1976–2016 |
| Siep Wyma | 1976–1977 |
| Dirkje Kelly | 1978–1998 |
| Murray McKenzie | 1978–1991 |
| Jim Weir | 1978– |
| John Kerse | 1980–2010 |
| Telford Watt | 1981–1991 |
| Lloyd Borlase | 1981–1986 |
| Ken Robb | 1981–1993 |
| Gordon Wilson | 1982–1987 |
| Graeme Gardyne | 1983– |
| Bruce Heslip | 1983–2013 |
| Alastair MacDonald | 1987–1992 |
| Hamish Mackay | 1987– |
| John Wilson | 1987–2017 |
| Richard White | 1988– |
| Elinor Collins | 1988– |
| Bruce Roy | 1988– |
| Basil Paterson | 1988–2009 |

| | |
|---|---|
| Neil Jackson | 1989–1999 |
| Gordon Collins | 1990–2015 |
| John Gardyne | 1991– |
| David Smith | 1991– |
| Paul Heslip | 1994–2009 |
| Andrew Tripp | 1996– |
| Andrew Clark | 1996–2001 |
| Douglas Dodds | 1998– |
| George Cook | 1999– |
| Jeremy McPhail | 2004– |
| Diane Cook | 2008– |
| Robert Erskine | 2010– |
| Peter Gardyne | 2013– |
| James Roy | 2013– |
| Philip McCallum | 2013– |
| Jonathan Gardyne | 2017– |
| Miriam Mackay | 2017– |

***

## List of Office Bearers

### Chairman

| | |
|---|---|
| Ron Paterson | 1967–1997 |
| John Moore | 1997–2001 |
| George Cook | 2001–2008 |
| Douglas Dodds | 2008–2016 |
| Graeme Gardyne | 2016– |

### Secretary

| | |
|---|---|
| George Simpson | 1967–1974 |
| Jim McNamara | 1974–1981 |
| Jim Weir | 1981–1988 |
| Elinor Collins | 1988–2008 |
| Diane Cook | 2008– |

### Treasurer

| | |
|---|---|
| Harry White | 1967–1989 |
| Richard White | 1989– |

# About the Author

Valmai Redhead is an emerging author who believes that compelling stories need to be shared. Stories, writing and mission have always been part of her life. Training as a librarian nurtured her love of books. She worked with Flo Brown to write her story as a missionary nurse in Nepal and *Precious Treasure, Clay Pot* was published in 2012. A recent visit to her daughter who is working in South Asia has added a new dimension to Valmai's appreciation of overseas mission. Valmai grew up in Dunedin but has lived in Southland for more than forty years, where she has pursued her love of writing, and has had work published in *NZ Memories* magazine and four anthologies. She is an active member of Calvin Community Church in Gore.

www.valmairedhead.com

www.ingramcontent.com/pod-product-compliance
Ingram Content Group UK Ltd.
Pitfield, Milton Keynes, MK11 3LW, UK
UKHW021051270726
13967UKWH00012B/545